Betty Crocker's

FABULOUS FISH AND SEAFOOD

Macmillan • USA

MACMILLAN
A Prentice Hall Macmillan Company
15 Columbus Circle
New York, NY 10023

Library of Congress Cataloging-in-Publication Data
Betty Crocker's Fabulous Fish and Seafood.

p.cm.

Includes index

ISBN 0-02-860281-1

1. Cookery (Seafood) 2. Cookery (Fish)
I. Title: Fabulous fish and seafood.

  TX747.B435 1995

641.6 '92—dc20   94–37683   CIP

Manufactured in the United States of America

10 9 8 7 6 5 4 3 2 1

Contents

Introduction

— ▣ —

Fish is gaining popularity as a light entrée that is extremely healthful, full of protein and low-fat. It's also versatile and easy to prepare for a fast-paced lifestyle. This great collection of recipes presents fish in its many delicious forms, from soups and salads to delicious main dishes, all of which fit today's emphasis on lighter eating and quick preparation.

Beginning with a chapter on main dish recipes, you'll find a dish to suit any need from a quick-to-fix dinner with Crunchy Oven-fried Flounder to a sophisticated supper of Herbed Broiled Bass or Orange Roughy with Red Peppers. Looking for a hearty seafood dinner? Whip up a quick Seafood Pizza, or try such family favorites as Crab Cakes, Quick Jambalaya or Southwestern Stir-fried Shrimp. Need a homey soup? Make classics such as Bouillabaisse, New England or Manhattan Clam Chowder or Shrimp Gumbo from our Soups chapter. In the following chapters you'll be inspired to use fish and seafood in pasta and salads. You'll never grow tired of dishes such as Creamy Scallops and Pasta, Scampi with Fettuccine, Marinated Shrimp Kabob Salad or Spicy Seafood Salad.

We have also included an entire chapter on grilling. Who wouldn't be tempted with fish grilled to perfection in such dishes as Mediterranean Snapper, Sole in Wine Sauce, Lemon Fish Steaks or Grilled Red Snapper with Vegetable Sauté? And if you're looking for great seafood, you can't go wrong with Grilled Seafood Kabobs, Grilled Texas Shrimp or Grilled Lobster Tail.

You'll find everything you need to know when it comes to purchasing, storing and preparing fish, from how to select the perfect fish to sauce and marinade suggestions that are sure to please. For good taste and good nutrition, making fish and seafood part of your regular eating plan is simple with *Betty Crocker's Fabulous Fish and Seafood.*

THE BETTY CROCKER EDITORS

Facts on Fish

FISH BASICS

Fish is increasingly available in its fresh form, but frozen and canned fish remain the most popular ways to purchase fish and seafood. (Canned tuna is the number one–ranked fish intake in the United States today.) Smoked fish is also growing in popularity.

Because fish are delicate and tender, avoid overcooking, which makes fish dry and tough. Cook until fish flakes easily with a fork. You can test this by inserting a fork at an angle into the thickest part of the fish and twisting gently. For food safety reasons, we recommend cooking to an internal temperature of 160°.

SELECTING FRESH FISH

- Eyes should be bright, clear and not sunken.
- Gills should be reddish pink, never brown.
- Seals should be bright with a sheen.
- Flesh should be firm and elastic; it should spring back when touched.
- There should be no odor.

SELECTING FROZEN FISH

- Package should be tightly wrapped and frozen solid with little or no airspace between packaging and fish.
- There should be no discoloration; if the fish is discolored, this may indicate freezer burn.
- There should be no odor.

LEAN FISH, FAT FISH

Fish is divided into three classifications: lean, medium-fat and fatty. Fish containing less than $2\frac{1}{2}$ percent fat are considered lean. These fish are mild-flavored with tender, white or pale flesh. Lean fish are best steamed, poached, microwaved or fried. Fish with $2\frac{1}{2}$ to 5 percent fat content are medium-fat fish. These fish are suitable for all cooking methods. Fish with a fat content greater than 5 percent are considered fatty fish and generally have a firmer texture, more pronounced flavor and deeper color. Fatty fish are best broiled, grilled, microwaved or baked.

Individual fish have different percentages of fat that vary with the season, stage of maturity, locale, species and the diet of each fish. You can substitute one type of fish for another of the same classification when preparing your recipes.

Lean	Medium-Fat	Fatty
Bass, sea	Anchovy	Butterfish
Bass, striped	Bluefish	Carp
Burbot	Catfish	Eel
(freshwater cod)	Croaker	Herring
Cod	Porgy	Mackerel,
Cusk	Redfish	Atlantic
Flounder	Salmon, pink	Mackerel,
Grouper	Shark	Pacific
Haddock	Swordfish	Mackerel,
Hake	Trout, rainbow	Spanish
Halibut	Trout, sea	Pompano
Mackerel, king	Tuna, bluefin	Sablefish
Mahimahi	Whitefish	Salmon,
(dolphin fish)		Chinook
Monkfish		Salmon,
Orange roughy		coho
Perch, ocean		Salmon,
Pike, northern		sockeye
Pollock		Sardines
Red snapper		Shad
Rockfish		Trout, lake
Scrod		Tuna,
Smelt		albacore
Sole		
Tilefish		
Tuna, skipjack		
Tuna, yellowfin		
Whiting		

BUYING SHELLFISH

Live shellfish can be purchased in the seafood section of the supermarket or at a seafood store. Cooked shellfish can be purchased frozen or in the deli or seafood section of the supermarket. Following are guidelines for amounts to purchase.

- For live clams, oysters and mussels, allow about 6 oysters or small hard-shell clams, or 3 large hard-shell clams or 18 mussels or soft-shell clams (steamers) per serving.
- Allow about $1/4$ pound shucked oysters, scallops, clams or mussels per serving. Oysters, clams and mussels can be purchased shucked in their own liquid.
- Raw shrimp can be purchased with or without shells. Allow about 1 pound whole shrimp, $1/2$ pound headless, unpeeled shrimp or $1/4$ pound headless, peeled shrimp per serving.
- Allow about $1 1/4$ pounds live or $1/4$ pound cooked crabmeat or lobster per serving.

SHELLFISH DONENESS

Avoid overcooking shellfish, which makes it tough and rubbery.

- Raw shrimp is pink and firm when cooked properly. The cooking time depends on the size of the shrimp.
- Live oysters, clams and mussels open when they are done.
- Shucked oysters, clams and mussels become plump and opaque. Oyster edges will start to curl.

- Scallops turn white or opaque and become firm. Again, the size of scallops will determine the cooking time.
- Boiled crabs and lobsters turn bright red when properly cooked.

SHELLFISH BASICS

- Live clams, oysters and scallops should have tightly closed shells. Shells should not be cracked, chipped or broken. To test if open shellfish are alive, tap the shell; live shellfish will close their shells when disturbed. Never cook dead, unshucked clams, oysters, mussels or scallops. Shellfish should have a mild odor.

- Shucked clams, oysters and mussels should be plump, surrounded by a clear, slightly opalescent liquid. Clams may range in color from pale to deep orange. Oysters are typically creamy white, but may also be tinted green, red, brown or pink. Mussels are light tan to deep orange.

- Shucked sea scallops are about 2 inches in diameter, and bay scallops average about $1/2$ inch in diameter. Shucked scallops have a mild, sweet odor and should look moist; they should not be standing in liquid or on ice. Sea scallops are usually creamy white and may be tinted light orange or pink. Bay scallops are also creamy white and may be tinted light tan or pink.

- Live lobster, crabs and shrimp should have hard shells and moving legs. Discard any that show no movement. A lobster will tightly curl its tail when picked up. Soft-shell crabs are actually hard-shell crabs that have molted and shed their shell, which happens an average of 3 times per year.

- Shrimp may be sold raw (also known as "green" with the heads on); raw in the shell without the heads; raw but peeled and deveined. They are usually sold by count or number per pound. Counts and descriptions vary and can be confusing, because sometimes shelled shrimp count is based on number per pound before peeling while other times it is based on number per pound after peeling. Ask at your grocery store for clarification, if necessary.

HOW TO USE NUTRITION INFORMATION

Nutrition information per serving for each recipe includes the amounts of calories, protein, carbohydrate, fat, cholesterol and sodium.
- If ingredient choices are given, the first listed ingredient is used in recipe nutrition information calculations.
- When ingredient ranges or more than one serving size is indicated, the first weight or serving is used to calculate nutrition information.
- "If desired" ingredients and recipe variations are not included in nutrition information calculations.

How to Fillet a Fish

To fillet a fish, turn fish on its side and make a cut back from the gills straight down to the backbone.

Turn the knife blade flat and cut the flesh along the backbone almost to the tail. (Except for the tail portion, the top fillet will be separated from the rest of the fish with the narrow rib cage still attached.) Without removing knife, lift the still-attached fillet away from backbone and entrails, and flip it to the right so the flesh side is on the top and the skin side on bottom.

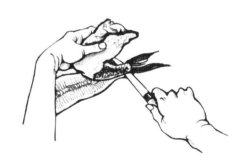

Cut the fillet away from the skin in one piece, sliding the knife between the skin and the flesh.

Cut the rib cage from the fillet. Turn fish over and repeat the above steps. If you like, scoop out the "cheek" of the fish (the little morsel of flesh under the eye) with a knife.

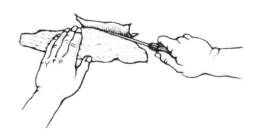

How to Eat a Lobster

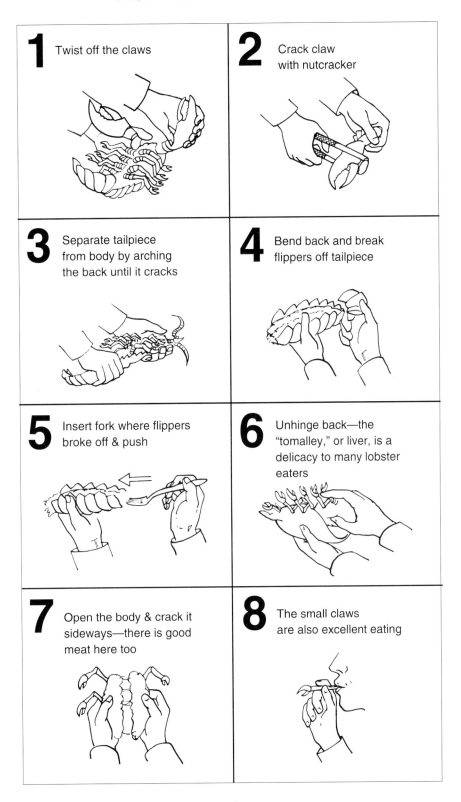

1 Twist off the claws

2 Crack claw with nutcracker

3 Separate tailpiece from body by arching the back until it cracks

4 Bend back and break flippers off tailpiece

5 Insert fork where flippers broke off & push

6 Unhinge back—the "tomalley," or liver, is a delicacy to many lobster eaters

7 Open the body & crack it sideways—there is good meat here too

8 The small claws are also excellent eating

Sensational Sauces

Fresh fish or seafood, broiled to perfection, is hard to top for flavor and appeal. Pair your fresh catch with one of these tantalizing toppers for a taste treat you won't soon forget.

Cocktail Sauce

1 cup ketchup
1 tablespoon finely chopped onion
1 tablespoon prepared horseradish
1 teaspoon Worcestershire sauce
$\frac{1}{2}$ teaspoon salt
3 drops red pepper sauce

Mix all ingredients. Refrigerate at least 1 hour.

About 1 cup sauce

Tartar Sauce

1 cup mayonnaise or salad dressing
2 tablespoons finely chopped dill pickle
1 tablespoon chopped fresh parsley
2 teaspoons chopped pimiento
1 teaspoon grated onion

Mix all ingredients. Refrigerate at least 1 hour.

About 1 cup sauce

Mushroom Dill Sauce

8 ounces mushrooms, sliced
$\frac{1}{4}$ cup margarine or butter
3 tablespoons flour
$\frac{1}{2}$ teaspoon salt
Dash of pepper
2 cups half-and-half
2 tablespoons chopped fresh or 2 teaspoons dried dill weed

Cook mushrooms in margarine in 2-quart saucepan over medium heat 3 minutes, stirring frequently; remove from heat. Stir in flour, salt and pepper. Gradually stir in half-and-half. Heat to boil over medium heat, stirring constantly. Boil and stir one minute, remove from heat. Stir in dill weed.

About 3$\frac{1}{3}$ cups sauce

Cucumber Sauce

1 cup finely chopped unpared cucumber
$\frac{1}{2}$ teaspoon finely chopped onion
1 tablespoon prepared mustard
$\frac{1}{2}$ cup mayonnaise or salad dressing
$\frac{1}{2}$ teaspoon salt
$\frac{1}{4}$ teaspoon pepper

Mix all ingredients. Refrigerate.

About 1$\frac{1}{4}$ cups sauce

Cilantro Pesto

1$\frac{1}{2}$ cups firmly packed fresh cilantro leaves
$\frac{1}{2}$ cup firmly packed fresh parsely
$\frac{1}{2}$ cup grated Parmesan cheese
$\frac{1}{2}$ cup vegetable oil
$\frac{1}{4}$ teaspoon salt
3 cloves garlic
$\frac{1}{4}$ cup pine nuts

Place all ingredients in food processor or blender. Cover and process until well blended

About 1$\frac{1}{4}$ cup sauce

Hollandaise Sauce

3 egg yolks
1 tablespoon lemon juice
$\frac{1}{2}$ cup firm butter*

Vigorously stir egg yolks and lemon juice in 1$\frac{1}{2}$-quart saucepan. Add $\frac{1}{4}$ cup of the butter. Heat over *very low heat,* stirring constantly, until butter is melted. Add remaining butter. Continue stirring vigorously until butter is melted and sauce is thickened. (Be sure butter melts slowly.) Serve hot.

About $\frac{3}{4}$ cup sauce

We do not recommend margarine for this recipe.

Menus

Quick Weekday Dinner
Crunchy Oven-fried Flounder (p.18)
Caesar Salad
Mashed Potatoes
Fruit Cup
Milk

Hearty Wintertime Fare
Manhattan Clam Chowder (p. 68)
Broccoli Quiche
Thick Slices of Whole Wheat Bread
Peach Cobbler
Wine or Warm Apple Cider

Company Is Coming Over
Flounder with Mushrooms and Wine (p.18)
Angel Hair Pasta or Linguine
Steamed Asparagus
Flaky Dinner Rolls
Cheesecake
Coffee or Tea

Light and Easy Lunch
Lemon Seafood with Pasta (p. 74)
Sliced Tomatoes with Vinaigrette Dressing
Rolls with Margarine or Butter
Seltzer Water

Fun Family Fare
Seafood Pizza (p. 34)
Garlic Bread
Tossed Salad
Chocolate Pudding or Ice Cream
Soda or Milk

South-of-the-Border Supper
Chips and Salsa
Grilled Texas Shrimp (p. 58)
Rice
Grilled Squash and Zucchini
Lemon Meringue Pie
Beer or Juice

Easy Summertime Cookout
Grilled Shrimp and Scallop Kabob (p. 60)
Potato Salad or Cole Slaw
Crusty French Bread
Watermelon
Brownies
Iced Tea

Baked Fish with Brown Rice-Vegetable Stuffing

1

Fish Main Dishes

Baked Fish with Brown Rice–Vegetable Stuffing

2 cups shredded carrot (about 2 large)
1 cup chopped onion (about 1 large)
1 cup uncooked regular brown rice
2 cups chicken broth
1 teaspoon Italian seasoning
¹/₄ teaspoon pepper
³/₄ cup shredded zucchini
1 pound fresh or frozen (thawed) sole or
    other lean fish fillets
Salt
Lemon pepper
1 medium tomato, cut into thin slices

Heat oven to 350°. Mix carrots, onion, rice, broth, Italian seasoning and pepper in 1¹/₂-quart saucepan. Heat to boiling; reduce heat. Cover and simmer about 35 minutes, stirring occasionally, just until rice is tender. Stir in zucchini. Heat to boiling; remove from heat.

Spoon rice mixture into ungreased rectangular pan, 11×7×1¹/₂ inches. Place fish fillets in single layer on top. Sprinkle with salt and lemon pepper. Cover with aluminum foil and bake 20 to 25 minutes or until fish flakes easily with fork. Place tomato slices on fish. Bake uncovered about 5 minutes or until tomatoes are heated through.

4 servings

SERVING SIZE: 1 Serving 310 Calories (35 Calories from Fat); Fat 4 g (Saturated 1 g); Cholesterol 55 mg; Sodium 790 mg; Carbohydrate 47 g; (Dietary Fiber 6 g); Protein 27 g; *% Daily Value*: Vitamin A 88%; Vitamin C 12%; Calcium 6%; Iron 10%

Sweet-and-Sour Fish

2 carrots, cut diagonally into thin slices
¹/₂ cup water
1¹/₂ pounds fish fillets, cut into 1-inch
**   pieces**
¹/₂ cup packed brown sugar
¹/₃ cup vinegar
2 tablespoons cornstarch
2 tablespoons soy sauce
1 can (15¹/₄ ounces) pineapple chunks
1 green bell pepper, cut into 1-inch pieces
Vegetable oil
Batter (below)

Heat carrots and water to boiling. Cover and cook until crisp-tender, 8 to 10 minutes. Pat fish dry with paper towels. Mix brown sugar, vinegar, cornstarch and soy sauce in 2-quart saucepan. Stir in carrots (with liquid), pineapple (with syrup) and green pepper. Heat to boiling, stirring constantly. Boil and stir 1 minute. Keep warm.

Heat oil (1 to 1¹/₂ inches) to 360°. Prepare batter. Dip fish into batter with tongs. Allow excess batter to drip into bowl. Fry 7 or 8 pieces at a time until golden brown, about 1 minute on each side. Drain on paper towels. Arrange on platter; pour sauce over fish.   **6 servings**

Batter

³/₄ cup water
²/₃ cup all-purpose flour
1¹/₄ teaspoons salt
¹/₂ teaspoon baking powder

Mix all ingredients.

SERVING SIZE: 1 Serving 440 Calories (180 Calories from Fat); Fat 20 g (Saturated 3 g); Cholesterol 60 mg; Sodium 940 mg; Carbohydrate 44 g; (Dietary Fiber 2 g); Protein 23 g; % *Daily Value*: Vitamin A 38%; Vitamin C 14%; Calcium 6%; Iron 10%

Fish and Chips

This favorite British dish is also a hit in the U.S.!

Vegetable oil
4 or 5 potatoes, cut lengthwise into
**   ¹/₂-inch strips**
1 pound fish fillets, cut into 2×1¹/₂-inch
**   pieces**
²/₃ cup all-purpose flour
¹/₂ teaspoon salt
¹/₂ teaspoon baking soda
1 tablespoon vinegar
²/₃ cup water
Malt or cider vinegar
Salt

Heat oil (2 to 3 inches) in deep fat fryer to 375°. Fill basket ¹/₄ full with potatoes; slowly lower into hot oil. (If oil bubbles excessively, raise and lower basket several times.) Use long-handled fork to keep potatoes separated. Fry potatoes until golden, 5 to 7 minutes. Drain potatoes; place in single layer on cookie sheet. Keep warm; repeat.

Pat fish dry with paper towels. Mix flour and ¹/₂ teaspoon salt. Mix baking soda and 1 tablespoon vinegar. Stir vinegar mixture and water into flour mixture; beat until smooth. Dip fish into batter; allow excess batter to drip into bowl. Fry 4 or 5 pieces at a time (see Note) until brown, turning once, about 3 minutes. Drain on paper towels.

Set oven control to broil and/or 550°. Broil potatoes 6 inches from heat until crisp, 2 to 3 minutes. Sprinkle with vinegar and salt. **4 servings**

NOTE: Do not use basket for fish.

SERVING SIZE: 1 Serving 305 Calories (145 Calories from Fat); Fat 16 g (Saturated 3 g); Cholesterol 60 mg; Sodium 790 mg; Carbohydrate 18 g; (Dietary Fiber 1 g); Protein 23 g; % *Daily Value*: Vitamin A *%; Vitamin C *%; Calcium 2%; Iron 6%

Fish Tempura

Tempura—an assortment of fish and vegetables dipped in batter, fried and served with a special sauce—has nearly as many fans in America as in Japan. Special tempura equipment can be purchased at department stores and oriental shops. Do not let the long list of ingredients discourage you from trying tempura; select, according to personal preference and recipe instructions, those that most appeal to your taste.

Shrimp with tails, shelled and deveined
Scallops, cut into halves
Fish fillets, cut into bite-size pieces
1 cup 1-inch pieces asparagus
1 cup 1/4-inch slices carrots or celery
1 1/2 cups cauliflowerets
1 1/2 cups 2×1/4-inch eggplant sticks
1 cup 2-inch pieces green beans, partially cooked
1 cup 2-inch pieces green onions
1 green pepper, cut into 1/4-inch rings
1 medium onion, sliced and separated into rings
1 bunch parsley
1 cup pea pods
1 sweet potato, cut into 1/8-inch slices
Vegetable oil
Tempura Batter (right)
Tempura Sauce (right)

Choose 1 pound seafood (about 4 ounces per person). If serving shrimp, make several crosswise slits on undersides to prevent curling. Choose 3 or 4 vegetables from selection above. Pat seafood and vegetables dry; arrange attractively on platter. Cover and refrigerate until serving time.

Heat oil (1 to 1 1/2 inches) in wok to 360° (see Note). Prepare Tempura Batter. Dip seafood and vegetables into batter with tongs, fork or chopsticks; allow excess batter to drip into bowl. Fry a few pieces at a time until golden brown, turning once, 2 to 3 minutes.

Drain. Serve with Tempura Sauce. **4 servings**

Tempura Batter

2 eggs, beaten
1 cup cold water
3/4 cup all-purpose flour
1 tablespoon cornstarch
1/2 teaspoon baking powder
1/2 teaspoon salt

Mix all ingredients with fork just until blended. (Batter will be thin and slightly lumpy.)

Tempura Sauce

1/4 cup chicken broth
1/4 cup water
1/4 cup soy sauce
1 teaspoon sugar

Heat all ingredients until hot. Serve in small individual bowls.

NOTE: A wok is recommended for this recipe because of its large surface area and slanted sides, which protect against splattering.

SERVING SIZE: 1 Serving 590 Calories (290 Calories from Fat); Fat 32 g (Saturated 6 g); Cholesterol 185 mg; Sodium 1660 mg; Carbohydrate 50 g; (Dietary Fiber 9 g); Protein 34 g; *% Daily Value*: Vitamin A 100%; Vitamin C 98%; Calcium 22%; Iron 42%

Herbed Broiled Bass

2 pounds bass or other lean fish fillets
$^1/_2$ teaspoon salt or seasoned salt
$^1/_8$ teaspoon pepper
$^1/_4$ cup ($^1/_2$ stick) margarine or butter, softened
$^1/_4$ teaspoon dried dill weed
$^1/_8$ teaspoon dried thyme leaves
$^1/_8$ teaspoon onion powder

Set oven control to broil. Grease broiler pan; place in oven to heat. If fish fillets are large, cut into 8 serving pieces. Sprinkle both sides of fish with salt and pepper. Place in broiler pan. Mix remaining ingredients; brush on fish.

Broil with tops 2 to 3 inches from heat 5 to 8 minutes or until light brown. Brush fish with margarine mixture. Turn carefully; brush with margarine mixture. Broil 5 to 8 minutes longer or until fish flakes easily with fork.   **8 servings**

SERVING SIZE: 1 Serving 170 Calories (90 Calories from Fat); Fat 10 g (Saturated 3 g); Cholesterol 50 mg; Sodium 260 mg; Carbohydrate 0 g; (Dietary Fiber 0 g); Protein 20 g; *% Daily Value*: Vitamin A 10%; Vitamin C *%; Calcium 2%; Iron 6%

Smoky Catfish

1 pound catfish fillets
2 tablespoons lemon juice
1 tablespoon soy sauce
$1^1/_2$ teaspoons liquid smoke
1 clove garlic, finely chopped

Spray rectangular baking dish, $11 \times 7 \times 1^1/_2$ inches, with nonstick cooking spray. If fish fillets are large, cut into 4 serving pieces. Arrange fish in baking dish. Mix remaining ingredients; brush over fish. Cover and refrigerate 30 minutes, brushing twice. Heat oven to 400°. Bake uncovered 20 to 25 minutes or until fish flakes easily with fork.   **4 servings**

SERVING SIZE: 1 Serving 100 Calories (10 Calories from Fat); Fat 1 g (Saturated 0 g); Cholesterol 60 mg; Sodium 350 mg; Carbohydrate 1 g; (Dietary Fiber 0 g); Protein 22 g; *% Daily Value*: Vitamin A *%; Vitamin C 2%; Calcium 2%; Iron 2%

Southern-fried Catfish

Pan-fried catfish used to be a southern secret, but it seems the rest of the country has caught on. Dipped in seasoned cornmeal and quickly fried, catfish served with hush puppies and coleslaw steals the show at southern fish fries. Found naturally in the Mississippi River and southern inland waterways, catfish are also farmed in several states of the Mississippi Delta.

Vegetable oil
$1^1/_4$ cups cornmeal
1 teaspoon salt
$^1/_2$ teaspoon ground red pepper (cayenne)
$^1/_4$ teaspoon pepper
6 small catfish (about $^1/_2$ pound each), skinned and pan dressed
$^1/_2$ cup all-purposed flour
2 eggs, slightly beaten

Heat oven to 275°. Heat oil ($^1/_2$ inch) in 12-inch skillet over medium-high heat until hot. Mix cornmeal, salt, red pepper and pepper; reserve.

Coat catfish with flour; dip into eggs. Coat with cornmeal mixture. Fry catfish, 2 at a time, until golden brown, about 6 minutes on each side. Keep warm in oven while frying remaining catfish. Garnish with lemon wedges, if desired.

6 servings

SERVING SIZE: 1 Serving 485 Calories (Calories from 170 Fat); Fat 19 g (Saturated 4 g); Cholesterol 195 mg; Sodium 570 mg; Carbohydrate 31 g; (Dietary Fiber 2 g); Protein 49 g; *% Daily Value*: Vitamin A 6%; Vitamin C *%; Calcium 4%; Iron 14%

Southern-fried Catfish

Flounder with Mushrooms and Wine

1 pound flounder or lean fish fillets
$^1/_2$ teaspoon paprika
$^1/_4$ teaspoon salt
$^1/_8$ teaspoon pepper
$1^1/_2$ cups sliced mushrooms* (about
    4 ounces)
$^1/_3$ cup sliced leeks
1 tablespoon reduced-calorie margarine
$^1/_3$ cup dry white wine
$^1/_4$ cup sliced almonds
1 tablespoon grated Parmesan cheese

Heat oven to 375°. If fish fillets are large, cut into 4 serving pieces. Arrange in ungreased square baking dish, 8×8×2 inches; sprinkle with paprika, salt and pepper. Cook and stir mushrooms and leeks in margarine until leeks are tender; stir in wine. Pour mushroom mixture over fish; sprinkle with almonds and cheese. Bake uncovered until fish flakes easily with fork, about 25 minutes. **4 servings**

1 can (4 ounces) mushroom stems and pieces, drained, can be substituted for the mushrooms.

SERVING SIZE: 1 Serving 165 Calories (65 Calories from Fat); Fat 7 g (Saturated 1 g); Cholesterol 55 mg; Sodium 280 mg; Carbohydrate 4 g; (Dietary Fiber 1 g); Protein 22 g; *% Daily Value*: Vitamin A 6%; Vitamin C 2%; Calcium 6%; Iron 6%

Crunchy Oven-fried Flounder

1 pound flounder or other lean fish fillets
$^1/_3$ cup sour cream
1 tablespoon lemon juice
$^1/_2$ teaspoon chile powder
$^3/_4$ cup finely crushed corn chips
2 tablespoons margarine or butter, melted

Move oven rack to slightly above the middle position of oven. Heat oven to 500°. Grease rectangular baking dish, 13×9×2 inches. If fish fillets are large, cut into 4 serving pieces; pat dry. Mix sour cream, lemon juice and chile powder.

Dip fish into sour cream mixture; coat with chips. Place in baking dish. Pour margarine over fish.

Bake uncovered 10 to 12 minutes or until fish flakes easily with fork. **4 servings**

SERVING SIZE: 1 Serving 205 Calories (110 Calories from Fat); Fat 12 g (Saturated 4 g); Cholesterol 70 mg; Sodium 190 mg; Carbohydrate 4 g; (Dietary Fiber 0 g); Protein 20 g; *% Daily Value*: Vitamin A 12%; Vitamin C *%; Calcium 4%; Iron 2%

Nothing Fishy Here!

Here are some handy tips for buying, cooking, and storing fish.

WHAT TO LOOK FOR WHEN BUYING

• Flesh of fin should be firm and elastic; it should spring back when touched.
• Frozen fish should be tightly wrapped and frozen solid with little or no airspace between the packaging and the fish. Any discoloration may indicate freezer burn.
• There should be no off-odor.

WHEN IS SEAFOOD DONE?

• Fin Fish: when fish flakes easily with fork or reaches 160° using a meat thermometer.
• Shellfish: when raw shrimp turns pink and firm; scallops turn white or opaque and become firm.

HOW SHOULD SEAFOOD BE STORED?

• Uncooked—Refrigerate tightly covered in original package 1 to 2 days. Freeze in airtight container up to 4 months; thaw in refrigerator.
• Cooked—Refrigerate tightly covered 1 to 2 days. Freeze tightly wrapped up to 2 months; thaw in refrigerator.

Crunchy Oven-fried Flounder

Garlic Cod

1 pound cod fillets
¹/₄ teaspoon salt
Dash of pepper
2 tablespoons margarine or butter, melted
1 tablespoon lemon juice
¹/₂ teaspoon onion powder
¹/₄ teaspoon paprika
5 large cloves garlic, finely chopped
2 tablespoons margarine or butter
1 tablespoon olive or vegetable oil
5 lemon wedges

If fish fillets are large, cut into 5 serving pieces. Sprinkle both sides with salt and pepper. Mix melted margarine, the lemon juice, onion powder and paprika. Dip fish into margarine mixture. Place in ungreased square pan, 9×9×2 inches. Pour remaining margarine mixture over fish. Cook uncovered in 350° oven until fish flakes easily with fork, 25 to 30 minutes. Cook and stir garlic in 2 tablespoons margarine and the oil over medium heat until garlic is brown; spoon over fish. Garnish with snipped parsley, if desired. Serve with lemon wedges. **5 servings**

TO MICROWAVE: If fish fillets are large, cut into 5 serving pieces. Sprinkle both sides with salt and pepper. Mix melted margarine, the lemon juice, onion powder and paprika. Dip fish into margarine mixture. Arrange fish with thickest parts to outside edges in ungreased microwavable dish, 8×8×2 inches. Pour remaining margarine mixture over fish. Cover tightly and microwave on high (100%) 2 minutes; rotate dish ¹/₂ turn. Microwave until fish flakes easily with fork, 2 to 4 minutes longer. Let stand 3 minutes. Place garlic, 2 tablespoons margarine and the oil in 2-cup microwavable measure. Cover loosely and microwave until garlic is brown, 4 to 5 minutes; pour over fish. Serve with lemon wedges.

SERVING SIZE: 1 Serving 195 Calories (Calories from 115 Fat); Fat 13 g (Saturated 3 g); Cholesterol 50 mg; Sodium 290 mg; Carbohydrate 2 g; (Dietary Fiber 0 g); Protein 17 g; % Daily Value: Vitamin A 14%; Vitamin C 6%; Calcium 2%; Iron 2%

Cod with Marinated Tomatoes

Good source of protein.

1¹/₂ cups chopped tomato (about 2 medium)
¹/₄ cup sliced green onions
2 tablespoons vinegar
2 tablespoons water
1 tablespoon capers
¹/₂ teaspoon salt
¹/₄ teaspoon red pepper sauce
1 pound cod fillets
1 teaspoon salt

Mix tomatoes, onions, vinegar, water, capers, ¹/₂ teaspoon salt and the pepper sauce in glass jar or bowl. Cover and let stand at room temperature at least 4 hours.

If fish fillets are large, cut into 5 serving pieces. Heat 1¹/₂ inches water and 1 teaspoon salt to boiling in 10-inch skillet; reduce heat. Place fish in single layer in skillet. Heat to boiling; reduce heat. Simmer uncovered until fish flakes easily with fork, 4 to 6 minutes. Remove fish with slotted spoon. Drain tomato mixture; spoon over fish. **5 servings**

TO MICROWAVE: Prepare tomato mixture as directed. Arrange fish with thickest parts to outside edges in ungreased microwavable dish, 8×8×2 inches. Cover tightly and microwave on high (100%) 3 minutes; rotate dish ¹/₂ turn. Microwave until fish flakes easily with fork, 2 to 4 minutes longer. Remove fish with slotted spoon. Drain tomato mixture; spoon over fish.

SERVING SIZE: 1 Serving 90 Calories (10 Calories from Fat); Fat 1 g (Saturated 0 g); Cholesterol 50 mg; Sodium 720 mg; Carbohydrate 3 g; (Dietary Fiber 0 g); Protein 17 g; % Daily Value: Vitamin A 4%; Vitamin C 8%; Calcium 2%; Iron 2%

Pompano in Parchment

Pompano is a delicate-flavored white-fleshed fish found in the warm waters of the Gulf of Mexico. When serving this Creole classic, it's customary to slash open the parchment packets in front of guests so they can savor the aroma and drama!

2 cups water
1/2 cup Chenin Blanc or dry white wine
1/2 teaspoon salt
1 medium onion, sliced
3 slices lemon
3 sprigs parsley
1 bay leaf
4 black peppercorns
4 pompano, trout or pike fillets (about
  1 pound)
Mushroom Sauce (right)
4 pieces kitchen parchment paper or
  aluminum foil, 12×15 inches
Vegetable oil
12 cleaned medium uncooked shrimp
  (about 1 cup)

Heat water, wine, salt, onion, lemon, parsley, bay leaf and peppercorns to boiling in 12-inch skillet; reduce heat. Cover and simmer 5 minutes.

Place fish fillets in skillet. Heat to boiling; reduce heat. Simmer uncovered until fish flakes easily with fork, 3 to 6 minutes. Carefully remove fish using slotted spoon; drain on wire rack. Reserve liquid in skillet for Mushroom Sauce.

Heat oven to 400°. Prepare Mushroom Sauce. Cut each piece of parchment paper into heart shape, about 14×12 inches. Brush oil over each heart to within 1/2 inch of edge.

Spoon 1/4 cup Mushroom Sauce on one side of each heart. Place 1 piece of fish on sauce. Arrange 3 shrimp on each piece of fish; spoon about 1 tablespoon sauce over shrimp. Fold other half of heart over top. Beginning at top of heart, seal edges by turning up and folding together; twist tip of heart to hold packet closed.

Bake on ungreased cookie sheet until paper puffs up and is light brown, about 15 minutes. To serve, cut a large X on top of each packet; fold back corners.   **4 servings**

Mushroom Sauce

Reserved cooking liquid
1 cup sliced mushrooms
3 tablespoons margarine or butter
3 tablespoons all-purpose flour
1/4 teaspoon salt
1/8 teaspoon white pepper
1/4 cup half-and-half

Strain cooking liquid. Heat to boiling; boil until liquid measures 1 cup; reserve. Cook mushrooms and margarine in 1 1/2-quart saucepan over low heat, stirring occasionally, until mushrooms are tender, about 5 minutes. Stir in flour, salt and white pepper. Cook over low heat, stirring constantly, until bubbly; remove from heat. Gradually stir in reserved liquid and half-and-half. Heat to boiling, stirring constantly. Boil and stir 1 minute.

SERVING SIZE: 1 Serving 340 Calories (200 Calories from Fat); Fat 22 g (Saturated 7 g); Cholesterol 95 mg; Sodium 610 mg; Carbohydrate 9 g; (Dietary Fiber 1 g); Protein 26 g; *% Daily Value*: Vitamin A 16%; Vitamin C 4%; Calcium 8%; Iron 10%

Parmesan-Basil Perch

1 pound ocean perch or other lean fish
    fillets, cut into 4 serving pieces
2 tablespoons dry bread crumbs
1 tablespoon grated Parmesan cheese
1 tablespoon chopped fresh or
    1 teaspoon dried basil leaves
1/2 teaspoon paprika
Dash of pepper
1 tablespoon margarine, melted
2 tablespoons chopped fresh parsley

Move oven rack to position slightly above middle of oven. Heat oven to 500°. Spray rectangular pan, 13×9×2 inches, with nonstick cooking spray. Mix remaining ingredients except margarine and parsley. Brush one side of fish with margarine; dip into crumb mixture. Place fish, coated sides up, in pan. Bake uncovered about 10 minutes or until fish flakes easily with fork. Sprinkle with parsley. **4 servings**

SERVING SIZE: 1 Serving 145 Calories (45 Calories from Fat); Fat 5 g (Saturated 1 g); Cholesterol 60 mg; Sodium 180 mg; Carbohydrate 3 g; (Dietary Fiber 0 g); Protein 22 g; *% Daily Value*: Vitamin A 8%; Vitamin C 2%; Calcium 4%; Iron 4%

Quick Coating Ideas

Try these quick coatings for whole fish or fillets when frying or baking:

Seasoned bread crumbs

Bread crumbs and Parmesan cheese

Bread crumbs and seasoning mix

Bread crumbs and dry salad dressing mix

Cornmeal and chile powder (or Cajun spice)

Crushed cornflakes or other cereal

Crushed corn chips

Poached Fish Dijon

1 pound cod or firm lean fish fillets
2 cups water
1/3 cup skim milk
1/2 teaspoon salt
1 lemon, peeled, thinly sliced and seeded
Dijon-Dill Sauce (below)

If fish fillets are large, cut into 4 serving pieces. Heat water, milk, salt and lemon slices to boiling in 10-inch skillet. Place fish in skillet. Heat to boiling; reduce heat. Simmer uncovered 8 to 10 minutes or until fish flakes easily with fork.

Prepare Dijon-Dill Sauce. Carefully remove fish with slotted spatula; drain. Serve fish with sauce.
4 servings

Dijon-Dill Sauce

2/3 cup skim milk
1 tablespoon Dijon mustard
2 teaspoons cornstarch
1 1/2 teaspoons chopped fresh or
    1/2 teaspoon dried dill weed
1/8 teaspoon salt

Heat all ingredients to boiling over medium heat, stirring constantly. Boil and stir 1 minute.

SERVING SIZE: 1 Serving 135 Calories (20 Calories from Fat); Fat 2 g (Saturated 1 g); Cholesterol 60 mg; Sodium 520 mg; Carbohydrate 5 g; (Dietary Fiber 0 g); Protein 24 g; *% Daily Value*: Vitamin A 4%; Vitamin C 4%; Calcium 10%; Iron 2%

Risotto with Sea Bass and Zucchini

Arborio is the traditional rice for risotto. Different brands of rice have different absorption levels and may require an additional 5 minutes cooking time or up to ½ cup of additional broth.

2¼ to 2½ cups chicken broth
½ cup chopped celery (about 1 medium stalk)
¼ cup finely chopped shallots (about 2 large)
1 teaspoon grated lemon peel
1 cup uncooked Arborio or other short grain rice
½ cup dry white wine or apple juice
2 teaspoons tomato paste
1½ cups chopped zucchini (about 1 medium)
1½ pound bass or other lean fish fillet, cut into 1½-inch pieces
2 tablespoons sliced green onions
1 tablespoon chopped fresh or 1 teaspoon dried dill weed
6 lemon wedges

Heat 1 cup of the broth, the celery, shallots and lemon peel to boiling in 3-quart saucepan; reduce heat. Simmer uncovered over medium heat about 10 minutes, stirring occasionally, until liquid has almost evaporated. Stir in rice, ¾ cup of the broth, the wine and tomato paste. Heat to boiling; reduce heat. Simmer uncovered 15 minutes, stirring occasionally.

Stir in zucchini, fish and ½ cup of the broth. Cover and simmer about 20 minutes or until rice is tender and fish flakes easily with fork, adding remaining broth, if necessary, to prevent sticking. Stir in onions and dill weed; remove from heat. Cover and let stand 5 minutes. Stir rice mixture. Serve with lemon wedges. **6 servings**

SERVING SIZE: 1 Serving 270 Calories (55 Calories from Fat); Fat 6 g (Saturated 2 g); Cholesterol 65 mg; Sodium 380 mg; Carbohydrate 29 g; (Dietary Fiber 1 g); Protein 26 g; *% Daily Value*: Vitamin A 4%; Vitamin C 10%; Calcium 4%; Iron 12%

Orange Roughy with Red Peppers

1 pound orange roughy or lean fish fillets
1 teaspoon olive or vegetable oil
1 small onion, cut into thin slices
2 red or green bell peppers, cut into julienne strips
1 tablespoon snipped fresh thyme leaves or 1 teaspoon dried thyme leaves
¼ teaspoon pepper

If fish fillets are large, cut into 4 serving pieces. Heat oil in 10-inch nonstick skillet. Layer onion and bell peppers in skillet; sprinkle with half of the thyme and half of the pepper. Place fish over bell peppers and sprinkle with remaining thyme and pepper.

Cover and cook over low heat 15 minutes. Uncover and cook until fish flakes easily with fork, 10 to 15 minutes longer. **4 servings**

SERVING SIZE: 1 Serving 135 Calories (25 Calories from Fat); Fat 3 g (Saturated 1 g); Cholesterol 60 mg; Sodium 100 mg; Carbohydrate 5 g; (Dietary Fiber 1 g); Protein 23 g; *% Daily Value*: Vitamin A 22%; Vitamin C 58%; Calcium 4%; Iron 10%

Orange Roughy with Tarragon Sauce

Tangy nonfat yogurt makes a zippy, low-calorie sauce.

1 pound orange roughy or other lean fish fillets
¹/₄ teaspoon salt
1 tablespoon lemon juice
¹/₂ teaspoon chopped fresh or ¹/₈ teaspoon dried tarragon leaves
Paprika
Tarragon Sauce (below)

Set oven control to broil. Spray broiler pan rack with nonstick cooking spray. If fish fillets are large, cut into 4 serving pieces. Place fish on rack in broiler pan. Sprinkle with salt. Drizzle with lemon juice. Sprinkle with tarragon and paprika. Broil with tops about 4 inches from heat 5 to 6 minutes or until fish flakes easily with fork. Prepare Tarragon Sauce; serve with fish.

4 servings

Tarragon Sauce

¹/₃ cup plain nonfat yogurt
1 tablespoon reduced-calorie mayonnaise or salad dressing
¹/₂ teaspoon chopped fresh or ¹/₈ teaspoon dried tarragon leaves
Dash of salt

Heat all ingredients over low heat, stirring occasionally, just until hot (do not boil).

SERVING SIZE: 1 Serving 125 Calories (25 Calories from Fat); Fat 3 g (Saturated 1 g); Cholesterol 65 mg; Sodium 400 mg; Carbohydrate 2 g; (Dietary Fiber 0 g); Protein 23 g; *% Daily Value*: Vitamin A 4%; Vitamin C *%; Calcium 6%; Iron 2%

Care of Fresh or Frozen Fish

Store fresh fish in the coldest part of the refrigerator; freeze fish you don't plan to cook within a day or two. Keep frozen fish solidly frozen. If any kind of frozen fish becomes thawed, use it right away.

To freeze fresh fish, clean and scale it, then wash under running cold water. Drain and pat dry with paper towels, then wrap tightly in freezer wrap. Or place in a freezer container and cover with cold water. Separate steaks and fillets with a double thickness of foil, then tightly wrap, label and freeze.

Thaw frozen fish in the refrigerator—only long enough for easy handling (about 24 hours for a 1-pound package). Do not thaw fish at room temperature.

To speed up thawing, immerse fish (in a sealed package) in cold water. Use the fish as soon as it is thawed, drying with paper towels before cooking. Fillets or steaks can be fried, broiled or poached before they are completely thawed; they will take a little longer to cook. After they are cooked, fish can be covered and refrigerated no longer than three days or frozen no longer than three months.

Orange Roughy with Tarragon Sauce

Trout Fillets with Almond Sauce

$1/4$ cup all-purpose flour
$1/2$ teaspoon salt
$1/8$ teaspoon pepper
1 pound trout fillets, cut into serving
   pieces
$1/4$ cup milk
Vegetable oil
$1/4$ cup ($1/2$ stick) margarine or butter
$1/4$ cup slivered almonds
Lemon wedges
Snipped parsley

Mix flour, salt and pepper. Dip trout in milk; coat with flour mixture. Heat oil ($1/8$ inch) in skillet until hot. Cook fish over medium heat until golden brown, turning carefully, about 5 minutes on each side. Remove trout to platter; keep warm.

Drain oil from skillet; add margarine and almonds. Cook over low heat until margarine starts to brown. Spoon over trout; garnish with lemon wedges and sprinkle with parsley.

4 servings

SERVING SIZE: 1 Serving 400 Calories (270 Calories from Fat); Fat 30 g (Saturated 5 g); Cholesterol 65 mg; Sodium 470 mg; Carbohydrate 8 g; (Dietary Fiber 1 g); Protein 26 g; % Daily Value: Vitamin A 18%; Vitamin C *%; Calcium 8%; Iron 12%

Salmon with Rosemary Sauce

1 teaspoon chopped fresh or $1/2$ teaspoon
   dried rosemary leaves
4 fresh parsley sprigs
3 peppercorns
$1/4$ lemon
1 can ($14^{1}/_2$ ounces) ready-to-serve
   chicken broth
1 pound salmon or other fatty fish fillets
$1/2$ cup half-and-half
1 teaspoon cornstarch
1 teaspoon chopped fresh or $1/4$ teaspoon
   dried rosemary leaves
$1/2$ teaspoon salt

Place 1 teaspoon rosemary, the parsley, peppercorns and lemon in cheesecloth; tie securely. Heat broth and cheesecloth bag to boiling in 10-inch skillet; reduce heat. Cover and simmer 5 minutes. If fish fillets are large, cut into 4 serving pieces. Place fish fillets in skillet; add water, if necessary, to cover. Heat to boiling; reduce heat. Simmer uncovered 5 to 10 minutes or until fish flakes easily with fork. Remove fish to serving platter and keep warm. Reserve $1/3$ cup broth mixture. Discard cheesecloth bag and remaining broth mixture.

Mix half-and-half and cornstarch. Heat half-and-half mixture, reserved broth mixture, 1 teaspoon rosemary and the salt to boiling in skillet over medium heat. Boil and stir 1 minute. Pour over fish.

4 servings

SERVING SIZE: 1 Serving 220 Calories (100 Calories from Fat); Fat 11 g (Saturated 4 g); Cholesterol 85 mg; Sodium 670 mg; Carbohydrate 3 g; (Dietary Fiber 0 g); Protein 27 g; % Daily Value: Vitamin A 6%; Vitamin C 4%; Calcium 4%; Iron 6%

Salmon with Mint Couscous

Mint Sauce (below)
1¹/₂-pound pink salmon or other medium-
    fat fish fillet, cut into 6 serving pieces
1 teaspoon grated lemon peel
¹/₂ teaspoon salt
¹/₄ teaspoon pepper
3 cups hot cooked couscous
2 tablespoons finely chopped fresh or
    2 teaspoons dried mint leaves

Prepare Mint Sauce. Sprinkle fish fillets with lemon peel, salt and pepper. Set oven control to broil. Spray broiler pan rack with nonstick cooking spray. Place fish on rack in broiler pan. Broil with tops about 4 inches from heat 5 to 6 minutes or until fish flakes easily with fork.

Mix couscous and mint. Serve fish over couscous with Mint Sauce. **6 servings**

Mint Sauce

³/₄ cup plain nonfat yogurt
1 tablespoon finely chopped fresh or
    1 teaspoon dried mint leaves
1 tablespoon cholesterol-free reduced-
    calorie mayonnaise or salad dressing
1 teaspoon grated orange peel
1 clove garlic, finely chopped (about
    ¹/₂ teaspoon)

Mix all ingredients.

SERVING SIZE: 1 Serving 235 Calories (55 Calories from Fat); Fat 6 g (Saturated 2 g); Cholesterol 65 mg; Sodium 440 mg; Carbohydrate 21 g; (Dietary Fiber 1 g); Protein 25 g; % Daily Value: Vitamin A 2%; Vitamin C *%; Calcium 2%; Iron 6%

Cold Smoked Salmon with Herb Sauce

If you don't have a platter large enough to hold the salmon comfortably, place it on a large piece of parchment paper. Twist both ends and tie with ribbon to match the colors on your table.

5- to 6-pound whole smoked salmon,
    smoked trout or whitefish
Herb Sauce (below)

Remove head, tail and fins from salmon. Carefully peel off skin. Place on large platter and serve with Herb Sauce. Garnish with fresh dill weed, watercress and lemons, if desired.

6 to 8 servings

Herb Sauce

1 cup fresh dill weed
1 cup watercress
1 cup plain yogurt
¹/₂ cup mayonnaise
1 tablespoon grated lemon peel
3 green onions, cut into 1-inch pieces

Place dill weed, watercress and green onions in food processor; cover and process until minced. Stir in remaining ingredients. Cover and refrigerate at least 1 hour to blend flavors. **1³/₄ cups**

SERVING SIZE: 1 Serving 295 Calories (145 Calories from Fat); Fat 16 g (Saturated 3 g); Cholesterol 50 mg; Sodium 1550 mg; Carbohydrate 2 g; (Dietary Fiber 0 g); Protein 36 g; % Daily Value: Vitamin A 8%; Vitamin C 4%; Calcium 6%; Iron 10%

Smoked Salmon–Broccoli Soufflé

1 small onion, chopped
$1/4$ cup ($1/2$ stick) margarine or butter
$1/4$ cup all-purpose flour
$1/8$ teaspoon pepper
$1/2$ cup milk
$1/2$ cup Chardonnay or dry white wine
3 eggs, separated
$1/4$ teaspoon cream of tartar
1 package (10 ounces) frozen chopped broccoli, thawed and well drained
4 ounces smoked salmon, flaked or chopped

Heat oven to 350°. Butter 1-quart soufflé dish or casserole. Cook and stir onion in margarine in 2-quart saucepan over low heat until tender. Stir in flour and pepper. Cook over low heat, stirring constantly, until bubbly; remove from heat. Stir in milk until blended; stir in wine. Heat to boiling, stirring constantly. Boil and stir 1 minute; remove from heat.

Beat egg whites and cream of tartar in medium bowl on high speed until stiff but not dry. Beat egg yolks in small bowl on high speed until very thick and lemon colored, about 3 minutes; stir into wine mixture.

Stir about $1/4$ of the beaten egg whites into wine mixture. Fold wine mixture into remaining egg-white mixture. Gently fold in broccoli and salmon.

Carefully pour into soufflé dish. Bake uncovered until knife inserted halfway between center and edge comes out clean, 60 to 65 minutes. Gently divide soufflé into portions, using 2 forks. Serve immediately.   **4 servings**

SERVING SIZE: 1 Serving 260 Calories (155 Calories from Fat); Fat 17 g (Saturated 4 g); Cholesterol 170 mg; Sodium 440 mg; Carbohydrate 14 g; (Dietary Fiber 3 g); Protein 14 g; % *Daily Value*: Vitamin A 36%; Vitamin C 22%; Calcium 10%; Iron 10%

Broiled Salmon with Hazelnut Butter

Salmon and hazelnuts are both native to— and favorites of—the Pacific Northwest. Fresh king salmon, largest of the Pacific salmon, and silver salmon, with its deep coral color, are especially prized. You'll find the delicate Hazelnut Butter a wonderful topping for fish, vegetables and poultry.

Hazelnut Butter (below)
4 salmon fillets (1 to $1 1/2$ pounds)
$1/2$ teaspoon salt
$1/8$ teaspoon pepper

Prepare Hazelnut Butter. Set oven control to broil. Grease shallow roasting pan or jelly roll pan, $15 1/2 \times 10 1/2 \times 1$ inch. Sprinkle both sides of fish with salt and pepper. Place in pan. Broil fish with tops 4 to 6 inches from heat 4 minutes; turn and spread each fillet with about 1 tablespoon Hazelnut Butter. Broil until fish flakes easily with fork, 4 to 8 minutes.   **4 servings**

Hazelnut Butter

2 tablespoons finely chopped hazelnuts
3 tablespoons margarine or butter, softened
1 tablespoon chopped fresh parsley
1 teaspoon lemon juice

Heat oven to 350°. Spread hazelnuts on ungreased cookie sheet. Bake until golden brown, 4 to 6 minutes, stirring occasionally; cool. Mix with remaining ingredients.

SERVING SIZE: 1 Serving 255 Calories (155 Calories from Fat); Fat 17 g (Saturated 4 g); Cholesterol 75 mg; Sodium 440 mg; Carbohydrate 1 g; (Dietary Fiber 0 g); Protein 24 g; % *Daily Value*: Vitamin A 16%; Vitamin C 2%; Calcium 2%; Iron 4%

Broiled Salmon with Hazelnut Butter

Sole in Tomato Sauce

$1/2$ cup sliced fresh mushrooms (about
　1$1/2$ ounces)
$1/4$ cup dry white wine
1 tablespoon chopped fresh or
　$1/2$ teaspoon dried thyme
1 tablespoon tomato paste
1$1/2$ cups chopped tomatoes (about
　2 medium)
$1/4$ cup chopped onion (about 1 small)
1 clove garlic, crushed
8 thin sole fillets (about 1 pound)
$1/4$ teaspoon salt

Heat mushrooms, wine, half of the fresh thyme,*
the tomato paste, tomatoes, onion and garlic to
boiling in 10-inch nonstick skillet; reduce heat to
medium. Cook uncovered about 10 minutes or
until slightly thickened.

Sprinkle fish fillets with salt and remaining
thyme. Roll up fish. Place on tomato mixture in
skillet. Cover and cook over low heat about 15
minutes or until fish flakes easily with fork.

4 servings, with about $1/3$ cup sauce each

*Use full amount of dried thyme: omit sprinkling thyme
on fish fillets.*

SERVING SIZE: 1 Serving 120 Calories (20 Calories from
Fat); Fat 2 g (Saturated 0 g); Cholesterol 55 mg; Sodium
260 mg; Carbohydrate 6 g; (Dietary Fiber 1 g); Protein
20 g; *% Daily Value*: Vitamin A 6%; Vitamin C 12%; Calcium
4%; Iron 12%

Vegetable-Sole Roll-ups

$1/2$ teaspoon salt
$1/2$ teaspoon dried dill weed
$1/4$ teaspoon pepper
6 sole fillets (about 2 pounds)
24 carrot strips, each about 3 × $1/4$ inch
　(about 2 medium carrots)
18 green bell pepper strips, each about
　3 × $1/4$ inch (about 1 medium green bell
　pepper)
$1/4$ cup Chenin Blanc or dry white wine
2 tablespoons margarine or butter
2 tablespoons all-purpose flour
$1/4$ teaspoon salt
$1/8$ teaspoon pepper
1 cup milk
$1/4$ cup Chenin Blanc or dry white wine

Heat oven to 350°. Mix $1/2$ teaspoon salt, the dill
weed and $1/4$ teaspoon pepper; sprinkle over sole
fillets. Place 4 carrot strips and 3 bell
pepper strips across one end of each fillet; roll
the fillets around the vegetable bundles. Place
roll-ups, seam sides down, in ungreased rectangular baking dish, 13 × 9 × 2 inches. Pour $1/4$ cup
wine over fish. Cover with aluminum foil and
bake until fish flakes easily with fork, about
40 minutes.

Heat margarine in 1$1/2$-quart saucepan until melted; stir in flour and remaining salt and pepper.
Cook and stir 1 minute; remove from heat. Stir in
milk. Heat to boiling, stirring constantly. Stir
in $1/4$ cup wine. Boil and stir 1 minute.

Arrange fish on warm platter; pour sauce over
fish. Garnish with fresh dill weed, if desired.

6 servings

SERVING SIZE: 1 Serving 180 Calories (55 Calories from
Fat); Fat 6 g (Saturated 2 g); Cholesterol 65 mg; Sodium
440 mg; Carbohydrate 8 g; (Dietary Fiber 1 g); Protein 24 g;
% Daily Value: Vitamin A 46%; Vitamin C 10%; Calcium 8%;
Iron 4%

Swordfish with Thyme-Apple Sauce

Swordfish has a wonderful meaty quality that is very satisfying. Fresh thyme scents a sauce with apple slices.

Thyme-Apple Sauce (below)
1 pound swordfish or lean fish steaks,
   $\frac{1}{2}$ to $\frac{3}{4}$ inch thick
2 tablespoons lemon juice

Prepare Thyme-Apple Sauce; keep warm.

Set oven control to broil. Place fish steaks on rack sprayed with nonstick cooking spray in broiler pan; brush with 1 tablespoon lemon juice. Broil with tops about 4 inches from heat 3 minutes. Turn; brush with remaining lemon juice. Broil until fish flakes easily with fork, 3 to 5 minutes longer. Serve with Thyme-Apple Sauce.

4 servings, with about $\frac{1}{2}$ cup sauce each

Thyme-Apple Sauce

2 tablespoons chopped onion
1 teaspoon vegetable oil
$\frac{1}{2}$ cup unsweetened apple juice
$\frac{1}{4}$ cup water
1 tablespoon snipped fresh thyme leaves
   or $\frac{1}{2}$ to 1 teaspoon dried thyme leaves
$1\frac{1}{2}$ teaspoons cornstarch
$\frac{1}{4}$ teaspoon salt
Freshly ground pepper
1 large unpeeled red eating apple,
   thinly sliced

Cook and stir onion in oil in 2-quart nonstick saucepan over medium heat until onion is softened. Mix remaining ingredients except apple slices; stir into onion. Heat to boiling, stirring constantly. Boil and stir 1 minute. Stir in apple slices; heat until hot.

SERVING SIZE: 1 Serving 180 Calories (65 Calories from Fat); Fat 7 g (Saturated 2 g); Cholesterol 60 mg; Sodium 190 mg; Carbohydrate 11 g; (Dietary Fiber 1 g); Protein 19 g; % *Daily Value*: Vitamin A 2%; Vitamin C 4%; Calcium 4%; Iron 12%

Sole Gratin

3 cups fresh mushrooms, sliced (about
   8 ounces)
$\frac{1}{2}$ teaspoon salt
$\frac{1}{4}$ teaspoon pepper
1 pound sole or other lean fish fillets
$\frac{1}{4}$ cup dry white wine
$\frac{1}{3}$ cup coarsely crushed zwieback
$\frac{1}{4}$ cup sliced green onions
3 tablespoons chopped fresh or
   1 tablespoon dried cilantro leaves
2 tablespoons margarine or butter,
   melted

Heat oven to 425°. Place mushrooms in ungreased rectangular baking dish, $11 \times 7 \times 1\frac{1}{2}$ inches. Sprinkle with half of the salt and pepper. If fish fillets are large, cut into 4 serving pieces. Arrange fish on mushrooms. Sprinkle with remaining salt and pepper. Pour wine around fish. Mix remaining ingredients; spread over fish. Bake uncovered 15 to 20 minutes or until fish flakes easily with fork and top is golden brown. **4 servings**

SERVING SIZE: 1 Serving 185 Calories (70 Calories from Fat); Fat 8 g (Saturated 2 g); Cholesterol 55 mg; Sodium 430 mg; Carbohydrate 8 g; (Dietary Fiber 1 g); Protein 21 g; % *Daily Value*: Vitamin A 8%; Vitamin C 2%; Calcium 2%; Iron 6%

Seafood Pizza (p. 34)

2

Shellfish Main Dishes

Seafood Chilaquiles Casserole

$^1/_2$ cup vegetable oil

10 flour or corn tortillas (6 to 7 inches in diameter), cut into $^1/_2$-inch strips

$^1/_2$ cup sliced green onions

$^1/_4$ cup ($^1/_2$ stick) margarine or butter

$^1/_4$ cup all-purpose flour

$^1/_2$ teaspoon salt

$^1/_4$ teaspoon pepper

2 cups half-and-half

1 canned chipotle chile in adobo sauce, finely chopped

1 pound bay scallops

1 pound shelled medium raw shrimp

4 slices bacon, crisply cooked and crumbled

Heat oil in 10-inch skillet until hot. Cook tortilla strips in oil until light golden brown, 30 to 60 seconds; drain and reserve.

Cook onions in margarine in 3-quart saucepan over low heat until tender; stir in flour, salt and pepper. Cook, stirring constantly, until mixture is bubbly. Remove from heat; stir in half-and-half. Heat to boiling, stirring constantly. Boil and stir 1 minute; reduce heat. Stir in remaining ingredients except bacon. Cook over medium heat, stirring frequently, just until shrimp are pink, about 9 minutes.

Heat oven to 350°. Layer half the tortilla strips in bottom of greased 3-quart casserole; top with half the seafood mixture. Repeat with remaining tortilla strips and seafood mixture; top with bacon. Bake until hot, 15 to 20 minutes.

6 servings

SERVING SIZE: 1 Serving 705 Calories (350 Calories from Fat); Fat 39 g (Saturated 11 g); Cholesterol 165 mg; Sodium 1080 mg; Carbohydrate 51 g; (Dietary Fiber 2 g); Protein 39 g; *% Daily Value*: Vitamin A 26%; Vitamin C 4%; Calcium 28%; Iron 38%

Seafood Pizza

Pizza takes on a whole new taste with this wonderful homemade pie!

Basic Pizza Dough for One Crust (right)
1 cup Simple Pizza Sauce (right)
12 medium raw shrimp in shells
**1 cup shredded mozzarella cheese
   (4 ounces)**
**$1/2$ cup shredded provolone cheese
   (2 ounces)**
8 flat fillets of anchovy in oil
$1/2$ pound bay scallops
$1/2$ cup chopped fresh basil
$1/2$ teaspoon pepper
4 cloves garlic, finely chopped

Prepare Basic Pizza Dough and Simple Pizza Sauce.

Place oven rack in lowest position of oven. Heat oven to 500°. Peel shrimp, leaving tails intact. Press or roll dough into 12-inch circle on lightly floured surface. Place on ungreased pizza screen or in 12-inch perforated pizza pan. Press dough from center to edge so that edge is thicker than center. Spread pizza sauce over dough to within $1/2$ inch of edge. Mix cheeses; sprinkle over sauce. Place shrimp, fillets of anchovy and scallops on cheeses. Mix basil, pepper and garlic; sprinkle over seafood. Bake about 10 minutes or until seafood is done and cheeses are melted.   **2 servings**

Basic Pizza Dough for One Crust

1 package active dry yeast
$1/2$ cup warm water (105° to 115°)
$1^1/4$ to $1^1/2$ cups all-purpose flour
1 teaspoon olive oil
$1/2$ teaspoon salt
$1/4$ teaspoon sugar

Dissolve yeast in warm water in large bowl. Stir in half the flour, the oil, salt, and sugar. Stir in enough of the remaining flour to make dough easy to handle. Turn dough onto lightly floured surface; knead about 10 minutes or until smooth and elastic. Place in greased bowl; turn greased side up. Cover and let rise in warm place 20 minutes.

Punch down dough. Cover and refrigerate at least 2 hours but no longer than 48 hours. (Punch down dough as necessary.)

Simple Pizza Sauce

**2 cans (28 ounces each) imported pear-
   shaped tomatoes, drained**
1 tablespoon chopped fresh basil
$1^1/2$ teaspoons dried oregano
1 teaspoon freshly grated Romano cheese
2 teaspoons extra-virgin olive oil
$1/4$ teaspoon salt
$1/4$ teaspoon pepper
4 cloves garlic

Place all ingredients in food processor or blender; cover and process until smooth. Use immediately or cover and refrigerate sauce up to 48 hours. Freeze up to 2 months. Thaw in refrigerator before using.

About 3 cups sauce

SERVING SIZE: 1 Serving 955 Calories (280 Calories from Fat); Fat 31 g (Saturated 13 g); Cholesterol 165 mg; Sodium 3550 mg; Carbohydrate 105 g; (Dietary Fiber 13 g); Protein 77 g; *% Daily Value*: Vitamin A 74%; Vitamin C 96%; Calcium 100%; Iron 86%

Seafood Crêpes

For convenience, make the crêpes ahead (see Do-Ahead Tip) and keep them on hand for carefree entertaining.

Crêpes (right)
6 medium mushrooms, chopped
3 tablespoons chopped green onion
3 tablespoons margarine or butter
3 1/2 cups (about 18 ounces) cooked
    seafood, cut into bite-size pieces
3 packages (3 ounces each) cream
    cheese, cubed
1/3 cup half-and-half
3 tablespoons snipped parsley
2 tablespoons sherry (optional)
1 cup shredded Swiss cheese
1/4 cup chopped green onion

Prepare crêpes; keep covered to prevent drying. Cook and stir mushrooms and 3 tablespoons green onion in margarine until onion is tender. Stir in seafood, cream cheese, half-and-half and parsley. Cook, stirring constantly, until cream cheese is melted. Stir in sherry.

Place about 1/4 cup filling on center of each crêpe; roll up. Place 8 crêpes seam sides down in each of 2 ungreased oblong baking dishes, 12 × 7 1/2 × 2 inches, or ovenproof serving platters. Sprinkle each with 1/2 cup Swiss cheese. Cover and heat in 350° oven until crêpes are hot, about 20 minutes. Garnish each dish with 2 tablespoons green onion.

8 servings, 2 crêpes each

Crêpes

2 1/4 cups all-purpose flour
3/4 teaspoon salt
1/2 teaspoon baking powder
3 cups milk
3 eggs
2 tablespoons margarine or butter, melted

Mix flour, salt and baking powder; stir in milk, eggs and margarine. Beat with hand beater until smooth. For each crêpe, lightly brush 8-inch skillet or crêpe pan with margarine; heat over medium heat until bubbly. Pour scant 1/4 cup batter into skillet; immediately rotate skillet until thin film covers bottom. Cook until top is dry and bottom is light brown; turn. Cook other side until light brown. Stack crêpes as they are removed from skillet; cool. (Cover crêpes with plastic wrap to prevent drying.)

DO-AHEAD TIP: Stack crêpes with waxed paper between each. Wrap and refrigerate no longer than 2 days or freeze no longer than 3 months. Thaw wrapped frozen crêpes at room temperature about 3 hours.

SERVING SIZE: 1 Serving 505 Calories (250 Calories from Fat); Fat 28 g (Saturated 14 g); Cholesterol 200 mg; Sodium 640 mg; Carbohydrate 35 g; (Dietary Fiber 1 g); Protein 29 g; *% Daily Value*: Vitamin A 34%; Vitamin C 4%; Calcium 34%; Iron 22%

Seafood Ragout in Puff Pastry Shells

1 package (10 ounces) frozen pastry
    shells
2 tablespoons margarine or butter
8 ounces mushrooms, sliced
1 tablespoon snipped fresh parsley
1 green onion, chopped
2 tablespoons all-purpose flour
$1/2$ teaspoon salt
$1/8$ teaspoon white pepper
$1/8$ teaspoon ground nutmeg
$1 1/2$ cups milk
8 ounces sole or flounder fillets, cut into
    1-inch pieces
8 ounces fresh or frozen raw shrimp,
    peeled and deveined
8 ounces scallops*
1 cup sour cream
1 to 2 tablespoons sherry

Prepare pastry shells as directed on package. Heat butter in 3-quart saucepan until melted. Cook and stir mushrooms, parsley and onion in butter over low heat 5 minutes. Stir in flour, salt, white pepper and nutmeg. Cook over low heat, stirring constantly, until mixture is bubbly; remove from heat. Stir in milk. Heat to boiling, stirring constantly. Boil and stir 1 minute. Stir in sole pieces, shrimp and scallops. Cover and cook 3 to 5 minutes or until fish flakes easily with fork and shrimp are pink. Stir in sour cream and sherry; heat through. Serve in pastry shells.

6 servings

If scallops are large, cut into quarters.

SERVING SIZE: 1 Serving 535 Calories (325 Calories from Fat); Fat 36 g (Saturated 16 g); Cholesterol 135 mg; Sodium 550 mg; Carbohydrate 27 g; (Dietary Fiber 1 g); Protein 27 g; *% Daily Value*: Vitamin A 16%; Vitamin C 2%; Calcium 18%; Iron 20%

Crab Legs with Vinaigrette

4 quarts water
1 tablespoon salt
2 pounds crab legs, sectioned into 2-inch
    pieces
2 green onions, thinly sliced
2 tablespoons chopped fresh parsley
2 tablespoons chopped fresh mint
3 tablespoons butter
$1/4$ cup Marsala or dry red wine
$1/4$ cup red wine vinegar

Heat water and salt to boiling in large kettle or stockpot. Add crab legs. Cover and heat to boiling; reduce heat. Simmer 10 minutes; drain. Let stand about 10 minutes or until cool enough to handle. Crack crab legs with nutcracker; remove meat with sharp knife.

Cook onions, parsley and mint in butter in 10-inch skillet over low heat 8 minutes. Stir in crabmeat, wine and vinegar. Cook uncovered over medium heat 5 minutes.

6 servings

SERVING SIZE: 1 Serving 125 Calories (65 Calories from Fat); Fat 7 g (Saturated 4 g); Cholesterol 90 mg; Sodium 600 mg; Carbohydrate 1 g; (Dietary Fiber 0 g); Protein 15 g; *% Daily Value*: Vitamin A 6%; Vitamin C 4%; Calcium 8%; Iron 4%

Maryland Crab Cakes

Carefully pick through the crabmeat to remove bits of shell and cartilage. For an irresistible meal, serve hot crab cakes with fresh lemon slices or top each with a dollop of tangy tartar sauce.

1 pound crabmeat, cooked, cartilage
   removed, and flaked (2¹/₂ to 3 cups)
1¹/₂ cups soft white bread crumbs
   (without crusts)
2 tablespoons margarine or butter, melted
1 teaspoon dry mustard
¹/₂ teaspoon salt
¹/₈ teaspoon pepper
2 egg yolks, beaten
Vegetable oil

Mix all ingredients except oil. Shape into 4 patties, each about 3¹/₂ inches in diameter. Refrigerate until firm, about 1¹/₂ hours.

Heat oil (1 inch) to 375°. Fry patties until golden brown on both sides, 4 to 5 minutes; drain.

4 servings

SERVING SIZE: 1 Serving 435 Calories (200 Calories from Fat); Fat 22 g (Saturated 4 g); Cholesterol 220 mg; Sodium 1000 mg; Carbohydrate 30 g; (Dietary Fiber 2 g); Protein 29 g; *% Daily Value*: Vitamin A 12%; Vitamin C 2%; Calcium 22%; Iron 20%

Crabmeat Roll-ups

These roll-ups are great for brunch!

1 can (6¹/₂ ounces) crabmeat, drained and
   cartilage removed
¹/₂ cup shredded Swiss or Monterey Jack
   cheese (about 2 ounces)
¹/₂ cup shredded zucchini (about 1 small)
¹/₄ cup finely chopped celery
¹/₄ cup finely chopped onion
3 tablespoons chile sauce
¹/₂ teaspoon salt
10 slices white sandwich bread
3 tablespoons margarine or butter, melted
Avocado Sauce (below)

Mix crabmeat, cheese, zucchini, celery, onion, chile sauce and salt. Remove crusts from each slice of bread. Roll each slice to about ¹/₄-inch thickness. Spoon crabmeat mixture across center of each slice of bread. Bring sides of bread up over crabmeat mixture; secure with wooden picks. Place roll-ups, seam sides down, in ungreased baking dish, 13×9×2 inches; brush with margarine. Cook uncovered in 350° oven until golden brown and hot, about 25 minutes. Prepare Avocado Sauce; serve over roll-ups.

5 servings, 2 roll-ups each

Avocado Sauce

¹/₂ cup plain yogurt or dairy sour cream
¹/₂ teaspoon salt
1 medium tomato, chopped and drained
1 medium avocado, chopped

Heat yogurt and salt just until warm. Gently stir in tomato; heat 1 minute. Remove from heat; carefully stir in avocado.

SERVING SIZE: 1 Serving 360 Calories (160 Calories from Fat); Fat 18 g (Saturated 5 g); Cholesterol 45 mg; Sodium 1050 mg; Carbohydrate 35 g; (Dietary Fiber 3 g); Protein 17 g; *% Daily Value*: Vitamin A 16%; Vitamin C 10%; Calcium 26%; Iron 14%

Deviled Crabs

This recipe tucks gently seasoned crab-meat back into the crab shells for an elegant first-course presentation. If you don't have crab shells, scallop shells or even ramekins are good substitutions.

1 cup soft bread crumbs (about 2 slices bread)
$1/4$ cup milk
2 cups flaked crabmeat*
$1/4$ cup margarine or butter, melted
$1/2$ teaspoon dry mustard
$1/8$ teaspoon ground red pepper
1 egg, beaten
1 green onion, chopped

Heat oven to 400°. Grease 6 of the largest crab shells or 6-ounce ramekins. Mix bread crumbs and milk in large bowl. Mix in remaining ingredients gently. Spoon into shells. Place shells in jelly roll pan, $15^{1}/_{2} \times 10^{1}/_{2} \times 1$ inch. Bake 20 to 25 minutes or until light brown.   **6 servings**

Boiled Hard-Shell Crabs (right) or 2 packages (6 ounces each) frozen crabmeat, thawed, drained and cartilage removed, can be used.

About Shrimp

Raw shrimp (heads removed) are greenish or pink and are sold frozen or refrigerated by the pound. One and a half pounds of raw shrimp will yield $3/4$ pound cooked (about 2 cups). Cooked shrimp (shells removed) are pink and are sold by the pound. Canned shrimp can be used interchangeably with cooked shrimp. Shrimp are a low-calorie bargain—there are only 100 calories in a 3-ounce serving.

Boiled Hard-shell Crabs

3 quarts water
12 live or frozen (thawed) hard-shell blue crabs

Heat water to boiling in Dutch oven. Drop 6 crabs into Dutch oven. Cover and heat to boiling; reduce heat. Simmer 10 minutes; drain. Repeat with remaining 6 crabs. To remove meat, grasp body of crab, break off large claws, and carefully remove meat from claws. Pull off top shell; reserve. Cut or break off legs. Scrape off the gills; remove organs located in center part of body carefully. Remove meat from body. Scrub reserved shells with vegetable brush before filling.

SERVING SIZE: 1 Serving 155 Calories (90 Calories from Fat); Fat 10 g (Saturated 5 g); Cholesterol 100 mg; Sodium 240 mg; Carbohydrate 5 g; (Dietary Fiber 0 g); Protein 11 g; *% Daily Value*: Vitamin A 8%; Vitamin C 2%; Calcium 8%; Iron 4%

Fried Clams

Vegetable oil
$1/2$ cup all-purpose flour
1 teaspoon salt
$1/4$ teaspoon pepper
1 pint shucked clams (about $3^{1}/_{2}$ dozen in the shell)
3 eggs, beaten
$1^{1}/_{2}$ cups dry bread crumbs

Heat oil (1 to $1^{1}/_{2}$ inches) in Dutch oven to 375°. Mix flour, salt and pepper. Cut large clams in half. Coat clams with flour mixture; dip into eggs and then coat with bread crumbs. Fry 1 to 2 minutes or until golden brown; drain on paper towels.   **6 servings**

SERVING SIZE: 1 Serving 365 Calories (170 Calories from Fat); Fat 19 g (Saturated 3 g); Cholesterol 135 mg; Sodium 670 mg; Carbohydrate 30 g; (Dietary Fiber 1 g); Protein 19 g; *% Daily Value*: Vitamin A 10%; Vitamin C 8%; Calcium 12%; Iron 40%

Deviled Crabs

Lobster with Chinese Vegetables

A little lobster goes a long way when cooked Chinese style. For dessert, try fresh pineapple cubes skewered on wooden picks.

1¹/₂ pounds frozen lobster tails
1 package (6 ounces) frozen Chinese pea pods
3 medium stalks bok choy
2 tablespoons vegetable oil
2 cloves garlic, finely chopped
2 thin slices gingerroot, crushed
1 can (8¹/₂ ounces) water chestnuts, drained and thinly sliced
1 can (8¹/₂ ounces) bamboo shoots, drained
4 ounces mushrooms, sliced
1 can (10³/₄ ounces) condensed chicken broth
2 tablespoons cornstarch
2 tablespoons soy sauce
1 teaspoon salt
1 teaspoon sugar
¹/₄ teaspoon white pepper
2 green onions, thinly sliced
Hot cooked rice

Cook lobster tails as directed on package; drain. Cut away thin undershell (covering meat of lobster) with kitchen scissors. Remove meat; cut into 1-inch pieces.

Rinse pea pods under cold running water to separate; drain. Separate leaves from bok choy stems; reserve leaves. Cut stems into ¹/₄-inch slices. Heat oil in 12-inch skillet, Dutch oven or wok until hot. Cook and stir garlic and gingerroot over medium heat until brown. Add pea pods, bok choy stems, water chestnuts, bamboo shoots and mushrooms. Cook and stir over medium heat 2 minutes.

Stir in ³/₄ cup of the chicken broth; reduce heat. Cover and simmer 1 minute.

Mix remaining chicken broth, the cornstarch, soy sauce, salt, sugar and white pepper; stir into vegetable mixture. Cook and stir until thickened, about 30 seconds. Tear bok choy leaves into bite-size pieces; add leaves and lobster to vegetable mixture. Heat until hot. Garnish with green onions; serve with rice.

SERVING SIZE: 1 Serving 195 Calories (35 Calories from Fat); Fat 4 g (Saturated 1 g); Cholesterol 15 mg; Sodium 850 mg; Carbohydrate 32 g; (Dietary Fiber 2 g); Protein 10 g; *% Daily Value*: Vitamin A 2%; Vitamin C 12%; Calcium 4%; Iron 12%

Steamed Mussels in Wine Sauce

24 large mussels (about 2 pounds)
2 tablespoons olive oil
¹/₂ cup chopped fresh parsley
4 cloves garlic, finely chopped
1 cup dry white wine
¹/₂ teaspoon salt
¹/₂ teaspoon pepper

Discard any broken-shell or open (dead) mussels. Wash remaining mussels, removing any barnacles with a dull paring knife. Remove beards by tugging them away from shells.

Heat oil in 12-inch skillet over medium-high heat. Sauté parsley and garlic in oil. Add mussels, wine, salt and pepper. Cover and cook 10 minutes. Discard unopened mussels. Drizzle liquid from skillet over each serving.

4 servings

SERVING SIZE: 1 Serving 165 Calories (70 Calories from Fat); Fat 8 g (Saturated 1 g); Cholesterol 35 mg; Sodium 330 mg; Carbohydrate 5 g; (Dietary Fiber 0 g); Protein 13 g; *% Daily Value*: Vitamin A 12%; Vitamin C 18%; Calcium 6%; Iron 40%

Steamed Mussels in Wine Sauce

Lobster with Sparkling Wine Sauce

4 quarts water
1 tablespoon salt
4 large fresh or frozen (thawed) lobster tails (about 1 pound each)
2 tablespoons butter
6 fresh pear-shaped tomatoes, peeled and chopped
2 green onions, sliced
1 cup Asti Spumante or dry white wine
2 tablespoons lemon juice

Heat water and salt to boiling in large kettle or stockpot. Add lobster tails. Cover and heat to boiling; reduce heat. Simmer 12 minutes; drain. Let stand about 10 minutes or until cool enough to handle. Crack shells with nutcracker; remove meat with sharp knife. Cut meat into 1-inch pieces.

Heat butter in 12-inch skillet over medium-high heat. Sauté tomatoes and onions in butter. Add lobster, wine and lemon juice. Cook uncovered over medium heat, stirring occasionally, 5 minutes or until most of the liquid is evaporated.

4 servings

SERVING SIZE: 1 Serving 220 Calories (65 Calories from Fat); Fat 7 g (Saturated 4 g); Cholesterol 90 mg; Sodium 460 mg; Carbohydrate 12 g; (Dietary Fiber 1 g); Protein 23 g; % *Daily Value*: Vitamin A 18%; Vitamin C 32%; Calcium 8%; Iron 8%

Quick Jambalaya

Although we greatly reduced preparation, we kept all the great taste in this Louisiana classic.

1 package (8 ounces) brown-and-serve sausage links
1½ cups uncooked instant rice
1½ cups water
1 can (14½ ounces) stewed tomatoes, undrained
1 package (10 ounces) frozen quick-cooking shrimp
¼ cup chopped onion (about 1 small)
½ medium green bell pepper, chopped
2 teaspoons chicken bouillon granules
1 teaspoon chopped fresh or ¼ teaspoon dried thyme
¼ teaspoon chile powder
⅛ teaspoon ground red pepper (cayenne)

Cut sausages into 1-inch diagonal slices. Cook in 10-inch skillet according to package directions; drain. Add remaining ingredients to skillet. Heat to boiling, stirring occasionally; reduce heat. Simmer uncovered 10 minutes, stirring occasionally.

4 Servings

SERVING SIZE: 1 Serving 530 Calories (170 Calories from Fat); Fat 19 g (Saturated 7 g); Cholesterol 150 mg; Sodium 1660 mg; Carbohydrate 64 g; (Dietary Fiber 3 g); Protein 29 g; % *Daily Value*: Vitamin A 10%; Vitamin C 22%; Calcium 10%; Iron 32%

Quick Jambalaya

Creamy Shrimp and Artichokes

**1 package (6 ounces) fast-cooking long
    grain and wild rice**
**5 ounces fresh mushrooms, sliced (about
    1³/₄ cups)**
¹/₄ cup margarine or butter
3 tablespoons all-purpose flour
¹/₂ teaspoon salt
³/₄ cup half-and-half
**2 packages (6 ounces each) frozen cooked
    shrimp, thawed and drained**
**2 jars (6 ounces each) marinated artichoke
    hearts, drained**
¹/₄ cup dry white wine
¹/₄ cup grated Parmesan cheese

Prepare rice as directed on package. Meanwhile, cook the mushrooms in margarine in 2-quart saucepan 3 to 4 minutes, stirring frequently, until tender. Remove mushrooms with slotted spoon; reserve.

Stir flour and salt into margarine. Cook, stirring constantly, until smooth; remove from heat. Stir in half-and-half. Heat to boiling, stirring constantly. Boil and stir 1 minute. Stir in shrimp and artichoke hearts. Cook about 5 minutes or until heated through.

Stir in mushrooms and wine; heat until hot. Sprinkle with cheese. Serve over rice.

4 servings

SERVING SIZE: 1 Serving 385 Calories (205 Calories from Fat); Fat 23 g (Saturated 8 g); Cholesterol 140 mg; Sodium 2 mg; Carbohydrate 26 g; (Dietary Fiber 2 g); Protein 21 g; *% Daily Value*: Vitamin A 28%; Vitamin C 6%; Calcium 18%; Iron 22%

Southwestern Stir-fried Shrimp

2 tablespoons lime juice
2 teaspoons cornstarch
¹/₂ teaspoon ground cumin
¹/₄ teaspoon salt
¹/₄ teaspoon pepper
**1¹/₂ pounds raw large shrimp, peeled and
    deveined (about 24)**
**1¹/₂ cups chopped yellow bell pepper
    (about 1¹/₂ medium)**
**1¹/₂ cups chopped red bell pepper (about
    1¹/₂ medium)**
**1 cup chopped red onion (about 1
    medium)**
¹/₃ cup chicken broth
2 cloves garlic, finely chopped
¹/₈ teaspoon ground red pepper (cayenne)
**2 tablespoons chopped fresh cilantro
    leaves**

Mix lime juice, cornstarch, cumin, salt and pepper in medium glass or plastic bowl. Stir in shrimp. Cover and refrigerate 1 hour.

Spray 12-inch skillet with nonstick cooking spray. Cook bell peppers, onion, broth, garlic, red pepper and cilantro in skillet over medium heat 2 minutes, stirring constantly. Stir in shrimp mixture. Cook 3 to 4 minutes, stirring constantly, until shrimp are pink.

6 servings

SERVING SIZE: 1 Serving 100 Calories (10 Calories from Fat); Fat 1 g (Saturated 0 g); Cholesterol 160 mg; Sodium 320 mg; Carbohydrate 6 g; (Dietary Fiber 1 g); Protein 18 g; *% Daily Value*: Vitamin A 26%; Vitamin C 62%; Calcium 4%; Iron 16%

Scallops and Mushrooms in Wine Sauce

Oven-to-table scallop shells (either authentic shells or porcelain reproductions) are available; or broil in individual ramekins or custard cups.

2 packages (12 ounces each) frozen scallops, thawed, or 1¹/₂ pounds fresh scallops
1 cup dry white wine
¹/₄ cup snipped parsley
¹/₂ teaspoon salt
2 tablespoons margarine or butter
2 cups mushrooms, sliced (about 4 ounces)
2 shallots or green onions, chopped
3 tablespoons margarine or butter
3 tablespoons flour
¹/₂ cup half-and-half
¹/₂ cup shredded Swiss cheese
1 cup soft bread crumbs
2 tablespoons margarine or butter, melted

If scallops are large, cut into 1-inch pieces. Place scallops, wine, parsley and salt in 3-quart saucepan. Add just enough water to cover scallops. Heat to boiling; reduce heat. Simmer uncovered until scallops are tender, about 8 minutes. Remove scallops with slotted spoon; reserve liquid. Heat reserved liquid to boiling. Boil until reduced to 1 cup. Strain and reserve.

Heat 2 tablespoons margarine in 3-quart saucepan until melted. Cook and stir mushrooms and shallots in margarine until tender, 5 to 6 minutes. Remove from pan. Add 3 tablespoons margarine; heat until melted. Remove from heat; stir in flour. Cook over low heat, stirring constantly, until smooth and bubbly. Remove from heat; stir in reserved liquid. Cook and stir 1 minute. Stir in half-and-half, scallops, mushrooms, shallots and ¹/₄ cup of the cheese; heat until hot.

Toss bread crumbs in melted margarine. Lightly brush 5 or 6 baking shells or ramekins with margarine. Divide scallop mixture among baking shells. Sprinkle with remaining cheese and the crumbs. Set oven control to broil and/or 550°. Broil 5 inches from heat until crumbs are toasted, 3 to 5 minutes.   **6 servings**

SERVING SIZE: 1 Serving 405 Calories (190 Calories from Fat); Fat 21 g (Saturated 6 g); Cholesterol 55 mg; Sodium 830 mg; Carbohydrate 23 g; (Dietary Fiber 1 g); Protein 32 g; *% Daily Value*: Vitamin A 28%; Vitamin C 4%; Calcium 30%; Iron 30%

Curried Scallops

3 tablespoons margarine or butter
1 pound sea scallops, cut in half
3 green onions, chopped
1 tablespoon all-purpose flour
1 tablespoon curry powder
¹/₂ teaspoon salt
¹/₂ cup chicken broth
¹/₂ cup milk
1 medium tomato, chopped (about ¹/₂ cup)
3 cups hot cooked rice

Heat 1 tablespoon of the margarine in 10-inch skillet over medium-high heat until melted. Cook scallops in margarine 4 to 5 minutes, stirring frequently, until scallops are white. Remove from skillet; drain skillet.

Heat remaining 2 tablespoons margarine in same skillet. Cook onions, flour, curry powder and salt over medium heat, stirring constantly, until bubbly; remove from heat. Stir in chicken broth and milk. Heat to boiling, stirring constantly. Boil and stir 1 minute. Stir in tomato and scallops. Heat about 3 minutes, stirring occasionally. Serve over rice.   **6 servings**

SERVING SIZE: 1 Serving 270 Calories (70 Calories from Fat); Fat 8 g (Saturated 2 g); Cholesterol 25 mg; Sodium 520 mg; Carbohydrate 29 g; (Dietary Fiber 1 g); Protein 21 g; *% Daily Value*: Vitamin A 14%; Vitamin C 4%; Calcium 12%; Iron 20%

Scallops with Red Pepper Sauce

Scallops with Red Pepper Sauce

1 large red bell pepper, cut into fourths
$1/8$ teaspoon salt
10 drops red pepper sauce
1 clove garlic, finely chopped
$1/4$ cup plain nonfat yogurt
1 pound bay scallops
$1/4$ cup sliced green onions
Cilantro leaves

Place steamer basket in $1/2$ inch water in saucepan or skillet (water should not touch bottom of basket). Place bell pepper in basket. Cover tightly and heat to boiling; reduce heat. Steam 8 to 10 minutes or until tender.

Place bell pepper, salt, pepper sauce and garlic in blender or food processor. Cover and blend on medium speed until almost smooth. Heat in 1-quart saucepan over medium heat, stirring occasionally, until hot; remove from heat. Gradually stir in yogurt; keep warm.

Spray 10-inch nonstick skillet with nonstick cooking spray. Heat over medium-high heat. Add scallops and onions; stir-fry 4 to 5 minutes or until scallops are white in center. Serve sauce with scallops. Garnish with cilantro.

4 servings
(with about 2 tablespoons sauce each)

SERVING SIZE: 1 Serving 150 Calories (20 Calories from Fat); Fat 2 g (Saturated 0 g); Cholesterol 35 mg; Sodium 380 mg; Carbohydrate 7 g; (Dietary Fiber 0 g); Protein 26 g; *% Daily Value*: Vitamin A 20%; Vitamin C 40%; Calcium 16%; Iron 20%

Savory Butters

Use these tasty butters to brush on fish occasionally during cooking or to top your favorite fish. Mix $1/4$ cup margarine or butter, softened or melted, and one of the following:

GARLIC: $1/2$ teaspoon paprika, $1/8$ teaspoon pepper and 2 cloves garlic, crushed.

HERB: 1 to 2 tablespoons chopped, fresh or 1 to 2 teaspoons dried herb (basil, chives, oregano, savory, tarragon or thyme), 1 teaspoon lemon juice and $1/4$ teaspoon salt.

MUSTARD: 1 tablespoon chopped fresh parsley, 2 tablespoons prepared mustard and $1/4$ teaspoon salt.

SESAME: 1 tablespoon toasted sesame seed, teaspoon Worcestershire sauce and $1/2$ teaspoon garlic salt.

PARMESAN: 2 tablespoons grated Parmesan, $1/2$ teaspoon dried basil, $1/2$ teaspoon parsley flakes.

LEMON-CHIVE: 2 tablespoons lemon juice, 1 tablespoon chopped fresh chives, 1 teaspoon grated lemon peel.

CHILE: $1/4$ cup chile sauce, 2 teaspoons mustard, $1/4$ teaspoon chile powder.

Grilled Shrimp and Scallop Kabobs (p. 60)

3

Grilled Seafood

———————◼———————

Orange-Honey Fish

2 tablespoons frozen orange juice
  concentrate, thawed
1 tablespoon soy sauce
1 tablespoon honey
1 tablespoon vegetable oil
$1/2$ teaspoon onion powder
1 pound cod, haddock or halibut fillets,
  $1/2$ to $3/4$ inch thick

Mix all ingredients except fish fillets; pour over fish in glass dish. Cover and refrigerate at least 1 hour.

Remove fish; reserve marinade. Cover and grill fish about 4 inches from medium coals, turning once and brushing 2 or 3 times with reserved marinade, until fish flakes easily with fork, 12 to 20 minutes. Cut into serving pieces if necessary. Garnish with orange slices, if desired.
                                   4 servings

SERVING SIZE: 1 Serving 155 Calories (45 Calories from Fat); Fat 5 g (Saturated 1 g); Cholesterol 55 mg; Sodium 340 mg; Carbohydrate 8 g; (Dietary Fiber 0 g); Protein 19 g; *% Daily Value*: Vitamin A *%; Vitamin C 10%; Calcium 2%; Iron 2%

Mediterranean Snapper

$1/2$ cup spaghetti sauce
2 tablespoons lime juice
1 teaspoon dried oregano leaves
$1/2$ teaspoon salt
1 or 2 cloves garlic, crushed
$1^1/2$ pounds red snapper fillets,
  $1/2$ to $3/4$ inch thick

Mix all ingredients except fish fillets; pour over fish in glass dish. Cover and refrigerate at least 1 hour.

Remove fish; reserve marinade. Cover and grill fish about 4 inches from medium coals, turning once and brushing 2 or 3 times with reserved marinade, until fish flakes easily with fork, 15 to 25 minutes. Cut into serving pieces. Garnish with lime wedges, if desired.   **6 servings**

SERVING SIZE: 1 Serving 105 Calories (20 Calories from Fat); Fat 2 g (Saturated 0 g); Cholesterol 50 mg; Sodium 400 mg; Carbohydrate 3 g; (Dietary Fiber 0 g); Protein 19 g; *% Daily Value*: Vitamin A 2%; Vitamin C 2%; Calcium 2%; Iron 2%

Grilled Red Snapper with Vegetable Sauté

Southwest Vegetable Sauté (including
   Lime Butter Sauce) (below)
8 red snapper or cod fillets (about
   5 ounces each)
$1/4$ cup vegetable oil
Salt and pepper

Prepare Southwest Vegetable Sauté and Lime Butter Sauce; keep warm. Generously brush fish fillets with oil; sprinkle with salt and pepper.

Grill over medium coals until fish flakes easily with fork, 10 to 12 minutes. Serve with Southwest Vegetable Sauté and Lime Butter Sauce.   **8 servings**

BROILED RED SNAPPER: Set oven control to broil. Place fish on rack in broiler pan. Broil with tops about 4 inches from heat until fish flakes easily with fork, 10 to 12 minutes.

Southwest Vegetable Sauté

Lime Butter Sauce (right)
$1/2$ cup finely chopped onion, (about
   1 medium)
2 cloves garlic, finely chopped
$1/4$ cup ($1/2$ stick) margarine or butter
4 very small pattypan squash (about
   4 ounces each), cut into halves
2 small zucchini, cut into $1/4$-inch strips
2 small yellow squash, cut into $1/4$-inch
   strips
1 medium chayote, peeled, seeded and cut
   into $1/2$-inch cubes
1 small red bell pepper, cut into thin rings
1 small yellow bell pepper, cut into thin
   rings
$1/2$ teaspoon salt
$1/4$ teaspoon ground red pepper
8 fresh squash blossoms, if desired

Prepare Lime Butter Sauce; reserve. Cook and stir onion and garlic in margarine in 4-quart Dutch oven until onion is tender.

Stir in remaining ingredients except squash blossoms. Cook over medium heat, stirring occasionally, until vegetables are crisp-tender; stir in squash blossoms. Serve with Lime Butter Sauce.   **8 servings**

Lime Butter Sauce

2 egg yolks
1 tablespoon lime juice
$1/2$ cup (1 stick) firm butter*
$1/2$ teaspoon grated lime peel

Stir egg yolks and lime juice vigorously in $1 1/2$-quart saucepan. Add $1/4$ cup ($1/2$ stick) of the butter. Heat over very low heat, stirring constantly, until butter is melted.

Add remaining butter. Continue heating, stirring vigorously, until butter is melted and sauce is thickened. (Be sure butter melts slowly so that sauce will thicken without curdling.) Stir in lime peel. Serve hot or at room temperature. Cover and refrigerate any remaining sauce.

About $3/4$ cup sauce

Margarine not recommended.

SERVING SIZE: 1 Serving 360 Calories (245 Calories from Fat); Fat 27 g (Saturated 10 g); Cholesterol 150 mg; Sodium 520 mg; Carbohydrate 6 g; (Dietary Fiber 2 g); Protein 25 g; *% Daily Value*: Vitamin A 30%; Vitamin C 26%; Calcium 4%; Iron 6%

Grilled Red Snapper with Vegetable Sauté

Grilled Sole and Peppers

3 medium bell peppers, cut crosswise into rings
12 ounces sole or other lean fish fillets
2 tablespoons margarine or butter, melted
1 tablespoon lemon juice
¹/₂ teaspoon garlic salt
Dash of pepper

Divide peppers among 3 pieces of heavy-duty aluminum foil, 18 × 12 inches. Place fish on peppers.

Mix margarine and lemon juice; drizzle over fish. Sprinkle with garlic salt and pepper. Seal foil tightly. Grill packets about 4 inches from hot coals 12 to 20 minutes, turning once, until fish flakes easily with fork and peppers are crisp-tender. Sprinkle with additional pepper or lemon pepper, if desired. **3 servings**

SERVING SIZE: 1 Serving 165 Calories (80 Calories from Fat); Fat 9 g (Saturated 2 g); Cholesterol 45 mg; Sodium 330 mg; Carbohydrate 5 g; (Dietary Fiber 1 g); Protein 17 g; *% Daily Value*: Vitamin A 16%; Vitamin C 56%; Calcium 2%; Iron 4%

Sole in Wine Sauce

This very elegant entrée is good for special entertaining.

1 pound sole fillets
¹/₂ teaspoon salt
¹/₂ cup thinly sliced fresh mushrooms
2 tablespoons margarine or butter
1 cup dry white wine
2 teaspoons instant minced onion
1 tablespoon cornstarch
¹/₃ cup cold water
2 tablespoons lemon juice
6 ounces cleaned raw shrimp
Snipped parsley

If fish fillets are large, cut into 6 serving pieces; sprinkle with salt. Cook and stir mushrooms in margarine until tender. Add wine and onion. Mix cornstarch and water; stir into wine mixture. Cook, stirring constantly, until mixture thickens and boils; boil and stir 1 minute. Stir in lemon juice.

Place each piece fish on 14 × 9-inch piece of double thickness heavy-duty aluminum foil; top each with shrimp. Turn foil up around fish; pour sauce over shrimp. Sprinkle each with parsley. Wrap securely in foil. Grill about 4 inches from medium coals, turning once, until fish flakes easily with fork, 20 to 25 minutes. **6 servings**

SERVING SIZE: 1 Serving 150 Calories (45 Calories from Fat); Fat 5 g (Saturated 1 g); Cholesterol 75 mg; Sodium 330 mg; Carbohydrate 3 g; (Dietary Fiber 0 g); Protein 17 g; *% Daily Value*: Vitamin A 6%; Vitamin C 2%; Calcium 2%; Iron 6%

Lemon Fish Steaks

¹/₄ cup lemon juice
3 tablespoons snipped chives
2 tablespoons vegetable oil
1 teaspoon dried dill weed
1 teaspoon paprika
¹/₂ teaspoon salt
1¹/₂ pounds halibut, salmon or swordfish steaks, ³/₄ to 1 inch thick

Mix all ingredients except fish steaks; pour over fish in glass dish. Cover and refrigerate at least 1 hour.

Remove fish; reserve marinade. Cover and grill fish about 4 inches from medium coals, turning once and brushing 2 or 3 times with reserved marinade, until fish flakes easily with fork, 10 to 15 minutes. Cut into serving pieces. **6 servings**

SERVING SIZE: 1 Serving 130 Calories (55 Calories from Fat); Fat 6 g (Saturated 1 g); Cholesterol 50 mg; Sodium 260 mg; Carbohydrate 1 g; (Dietary Fiber 0 g); Protein 18 g; *% Daily Value*: Vitamin A 4%; Vitamin C 2%; Calcium 2%; Iron 2%

Grilled Sole and Peppers

Grilled Salmon with Mint Marinade

4 small salmon steaks, ³/₄ inch thick (about 1¹/₂ pounds)
¹/₂ cup chopped fresh mint
¹/₂ cup olive oil
3 tablespoons lemon juice
¹/₂ teaspoon salt
¹/₂ teaspoon pepper
1 clove garlic, finely chopped
1 bay leaf

Place salmon steaks in ungreased rectangular baking dish, 11×7×1¹/₂ inches. Beat remaining ingredients except bay leaf thoroughly; stir in bay leaf and drizzle over fish. Cover and refrigerate 1 hour, turning fish over after 30 minutes. Remove fish from marinade; reserve marinade.

Grill fish uncovered about 4 inches from hot coals, turning over once and brushing with marinade frequently, 10 to 15 minutes or until fish flakes easily with fork. Heat remaining marinade to rolling boil; remove bay leaf. Serve marinade with fish. **4 servings**

BROILED SALMON WITH MINT MARINADE: Marinate fish as directed above. Set oven control to broil. Place fish on rack in broiler pan. Broil with tops about 4 inches from heat about 5 minutes, brushing fish with marinade frequently, until light brown. Turn carefully; brush with marinade. Broil 4 to 6 minutes longer, brushing with marinade frequently, until fish flakes easily with fork.

SERVING SIZE: 1 Serving 445 Calories (315 Calories from Fat); Fat 35 g (Saturated 6 g); Cholesterol 95 mg; Sodium 350 mg; Carbohydrate 1 g; (Dietary Fiber 0 g); Protein 31 g; % Daily Value: Vitamin A 4%; Vitamin C 4%; Calcium 2%; Iron 6%

Smoked Salmon

2 limes, thinly sliced
1 lemon, thinly sliced
3 pounds salmon steaks, 1 inch thick
¹/₂ cup margarine or butter, melted
1 teaspoon curry powder
¹/₂ teaspoon salt
¹/₄ teaspoon pepper

Soak 3 cups wood chips in water about 30 minutes. Form an 18-inch square pan from double thickness heavy-duty aluminum foil. Arrange lime and lemon slices in pan; place fish on slices. Mix margarine and curry powder; pour over fish. Sprinkle with salt and pepper. Arrange hot coals around edge of firebox. Drain chips; add to hot coals. Place foil pan on grill about 4 inches from coals; cover and grill until fish flakes easily with a fork, 40 to 50 minutes. **6 servings**

SERVING SIZE: 1 Serving 405 Calories (235 Calories from Fat); Fat 26 g (Saturated 7 g); Cholesterol 125 mg; Sodium 470 mg; Carbohydrate 3 g; (Dietary Fiber 1 g); Protein 41 g; % Daily Value: Vitamin A 26%; Vitamin C 14%; Calcium 4%; Iron 8%

Spicy Halibut Steaks

¹/₂ cup (1 stick) margarine or butter, melted
1¹/₂ teaspoons salt
2 teaspoons lemon juice
1 teaspoon prepared spicy mustard
3 pounds halibut or other lean fish steaks, each ³/₄ inch thick

Lightly grease grill. Mix all ingredients except fish steaks. Grill fish 4 inches from medium coals 6 to 8 minutes on each side, brushing frequently with margarine mixture, until fish flakes easily with fork. Garnish with lemon wedges and chopped fresh parsley, if desired. **6 servings**

SERVING SIZE: 1 Serving 295 Calories (155 Calories from Fat); Fat 17 g (Saturated 4 g); Cholesterol 100 mg; Sodium 870 mg; Carbohydrate 0 g; (Dietary Fiber 0 g); Protein 35 g; % Daily Value: Vitamin A 22%; Vitamin C *%; Calcium 2%; Iron 2%

Grilled Salmon with Mint Marinade

Stuffed Fish

Impress your guests by grilling this stuffed whole fish.

8- to 10-pound salmon, cod or lake trout, cleaned
Salt
Pepper
Garden Vegetable Stuffing (below)
$1/2$ cup margarine or butter, melted
$1/4$ cup lemon juice
Vegetable oil

Sprinkle cavity of fish with salt and pepper; spoon Garden Vegetable Stuffing into cavity. Secure with skewers and lace with string.

Mix margarine and lemon juice; reserve. Brush fish with oil; place in hinged wire grill basket. Cover and grill about 4 inches from medium coals, turning basket 3 times and brushing fish occasionally with reserved lemon juice mixture, until fish flakes easily with fork, 45 to 60 minutes. **20 to 24 servings**

Garden Vegetable Stuffing

1 cup finely chopped onion (about 1 large)
$1/4$ cup margarine or butter
2 cups dry bread cubes
1 cup coarsely shredded carrot
1 cup chopped mushrooms
1 tablespoon plus $1 1/2$ teaspoons lemon juice
1 egg
1 clove garlic, finely chopped
2 teaspoons salt
$1/4$ teaspoon dried marjoram leaves
$1/4$ teaspoon pepper

Cook and stir onion in margarine until onion is tender; toss with remaining ingredients.

SERVING SIZE: 1 Serving 285 Calories (125 Calories from Fat); Fat 14 g (Saturated 4 g); Cholesterol 110 mg; Sodium 640 mg; Carbohydrate 7 g; (Dietary Fiber 1 g); Protein 34 g; *% Daily Value*: Vitamin A 20%; Vitamin C 20%; Calcium 4%; Iron 8%

Confetti Fish

This recipe is very colorful and easy to prepare.

2 slices bacon, cut in $1/2$-inch pieces
3 green onions, cut into $3/4$-inch pieces
1 green pepper, cut into $3/4$-inch pieces
1 stalk celery, cut into $3/4$-inch pieces
1 medium tomato, cut into $3/4$-inch pieces
$1/2$ teaspoon salt
$1/8$ teaspoon pepper
14 ounces frozen pike fillets, thawed
1 tablespoon plus 1 teaspoon lemon juice

Cook and stir bacon, onions, green pepper and celery until vegetables are crisp-tender, 3 to 5 minutes. Stir in tomato, salt and pepper; remove from heat. Divide fish fillets among four 12-inch squares of heavy-duty aluminum foil. Sprinkle each fillet with 1 teaspoon lemon juice; top each with about $1/2$ cup bacon-vegetable mixture. Wrap securely in foil.

Grill packets about 4 inches from hot coals, turning once, until fish flakes easily with fork, 20 to 30 minutes. **4 servings**

SERVING SIZE: 1 Serving 125 Calories (25 Calories from Fat); Fat 3 g (Saturated 1 g); Cholesterol 55 mg; Sodium 420 mg; Carbohydrate 4 g; (Dietary Fiber 1 g); Protein 21 g; *% Daily Value*: Vitamin A 4%; Vitamin C 23%; Calcium 2%; Iron 4%

Whitefish with Stuffing

If you have any extra rice stuffing mixture, heat it in a covered aluminum foil pan next to the fish on the grill.

3 cups cooked rice
¹/₂ cup mayonnaise or salad dressing
¹/₃ cup chopped green onions
1 can (8 ounces) sliced water chestnuts, drained
1 jar (2 ounces) diced pimiento, drained
³/₄ teaspoon salt
¹/₄ teaspoon pepper
1 whole whitefish (2¹/₂ to 3 pounds), dressed
¹/₄ cup margarine or butter, melted

Lightly grease hinged wire grill basket. Mix all ingredients except fish and margarine. Stuff fish with rice mixture. Fasten opening with skewers; lace with string. Place fish in basket. Grill 5 inches from medium coals 50 minutes, turning once and brushing frequently with margarine, until fish flakes easily with fork. Garnish with lemon wedges, if desired. **6 servings**

SERVING SIZE: 1 Serving 585 Calories (315 Calories from Fat); Fat 35 g (Saturated 6 g); Cholesterol 120 mg; Sodium 550 mg; Carbohydrate 28 g; (Dietary Fiber 1 g); Protein 41 g; *% Daily Value*: Vitamin A 16%; Vitamin C 6%; Calcium 4%; Iron 16%

Teriyaki Fish

1¹/₂ pounds cod, haddock or halibut fillets, about 1 inch thick
¹/₄ cup lemon juice
2 tablespoons soy sauce
1 tablespoon vegetable oil
2 cloves garlic, crushed

If fish fillets are large, cut into 6 serving pieces. Mix all ingredients except fish; pour over fish in glass dish. Cover and refrigerate as least 1 hour.

Remove fish; reserve marinade. Cover and grill fish about 4 inches from medium coals, turning once and brushing occasionally with reserved marinade, until fish flakes easily with fork, 12 to 20 minutes. Cut into serving pieces, if necessary. Serve with lemon wedges, if desired.

6 servings

SERVING SIZE: 1 Serving 130 Calories (35 Calories from Fat); Fat 4 g (Saturated 1 g); Cholesterol 60 mg; Sodium 440 mg; Carbohydrate 2 g; (Dietary Fiber 0 g); Protein 22 g; *% Daily Value*: Vitamin A *%; Vitamin C 2%; Calcium 2%; Iron 2%

Crab-Stuffed Trout

An elegant stuffing for your very special catch.

6 rainbow trout (8 ounces each dressed weight)
Salt
1 can (7³/₄ ounces) crabmeat, drained and cartilage removed
¹/₂ cup finely chopped water chestnuts
¹/₄ cup dry bread crumbs
¹/₄ cup mayonnaise or salad dressing
¹/₂ teaspoon dried tarragon leaves
¹/₄ cup margarine or butter, melted
1 tablespoon lemon juice

Sprinkle cavities of fish lightly with salt. Mix crabmeat, water chestnuts, bread crumbs, mayonnaise and tarragon; toss. Spoon into fish cavities; secure with skewers, if necessary.

Mix margarine and lemon juice; reserve. Place fish in well-greased hinged wire grill basket. Cover and grill about 4 inches from medium coals, turning basket once and brushing fish frequently with reserved lemon juice mixture, until fish flakes easily with fork, 16 to 20 minutes. **6 servings**

SERVING SIZE: 1 Serving 490 Calories (250 Calories from Fat); Fat 28 g (Saturated 7 g); Cholesterol 180 mg; Sodium 770 mg; Carbohydrate 5 g; (Dietary Fiber 0 g); Protein 55 g; *% Daily Value*: Vitamin A 18%; Vitamin C 4%; Calcium 6%; Iron 12%

Grilled Texas Shrimp

¹/₄ **cup vegetable oil**
¹/₄ **cup tequila**
¹/₄ **cup red wine vinegar**
2 **tablespoons lime juice**
1 **tablespoon ground red chiles**
¹/₂ **teaspoon salt**
2 **cloves garlic, finely chopped**
1 **red bell pepper, finely chopped**
24 **large raw shrimp, peeled and deveined**
  (leave tails intact)

Mix all ingredients except shrimp in shallow glass or plastic dish; stir in shrimp. Cover and refrigerate 1 hour.

Remove shrimp from marinade; reserve marinade. Thread 4 shrimp on each of six 8-inch metal skewers. Grill over medium coals, turning once, until pink, 2 to 3 minutes on each side.

Heat marinade to boiling in nonaluminum saucepan; reduce heat to low. Simmer uncovered until bell pepper is tender, about 5 minutes. Serve with shrimp.   **6 servings**

BROILED TEXAS SHRIMP: Set oven control to broil. Place skewered shrimp on rack in broiler pan. Broil with tops about 4 inches from heat, turning once, until pink, 2 to 3 minutes on each side.

SERVING SIZE: 1 Serving 125 Calories (90 Calories from Fat); Fat 10 g (Saturated 2 g); Cholesterol 55 mg; Sodium 240 mg; Carbohydrate 3 g; (Dietary Fiber 0 g); Protein 6 g; *% Daily Value*: Vitamin A 16%; Vitamin C 20%; Calcium 2%; Iron 6%

Marinade Magic

Marinades give a special flavor to fish. Choose one of these delicious marinades for fish-grilling perfection!

- Marinate in covered nonmetal dish or sealed plastic bag.
- Turn fish (or bag) occasionally so all sides are covered with marinade.
- Refrigerate the marinating fish at least one hour, no longer than 24. Do not marinate at room temperature.
- Baste fish with marinade during grilling (about 10 minutes per inch of thickness) to keep moist and flavorful.

Herb Marinade

¹/₂ **cup lemon juice**
¹/₄ **cup vegetable oil**
¹/₂ **teaspoon salt**
¹/₂ **teaspoon celery salt**
¹/₂ **teaspoon dried thyme**
¹/₂ **teaspoon dried oregano**
¹/₂ **teaspoon dried rosemary (crushed)**
1 **medium onion, chopped**
1 **clove garlic, crushed**

Mix all ingredients.   **1 cup marinade**

Tangy Lemon Marinade

¹/₂ **cup lemon juice**
¹/₂ **cup vegetable oil**
¹/₃ **cup white or red wine**
2 **tablespoons grated Parmesan cheese**
2 **teaspoons sugar**
¹/₂ **teaspoon garlic salt**
¹/₂ **teaspoon pepper**
¹/₂ **teaspoon dried thyme**

Shake all ingredients in tightly covered container.

About 1¹/₃ cup marinade

Grilled Texas Shrimp

Grilled Seafood Kabobs

Marinade (below)
4 ounces salmon steak, cut into 1-inch cubes
4 ounces monkfish, cut into 1-inch cubes
4 ounces rockfish, cut into 1-inch cubes
12 medium raw shrimp in shells
4 small squid (calamari), cleaned
8 fresh large mushroom caps
1 large red bell pepper, cut into 1½-inch pieces
4 green onions, cut into 1-inch pieces
8 fresh or dried bay leaves

Prepare Marinade; reserve. Alternate fish, shrimp, squid, mushrooms, bell pepper, onions and bay leaves on each of four 12-inch metal skewers. Place kabobs in ungreased rectangular baking dish 13×9×2 inches. Drizzle Marinade over kabobs. Cover and refrigerate 45 minutes. Remove kabobs from Marinade; reserve Marinade.

Grill kabobs uncovered about 4 inches from hot coals 10 minutes, turning once and brushing with reserved Marinade occasionally, until fish flakes easily with fork. Discard bay leaves.

4 servings

Marinade

½ cup olive oil
1 tablespoon chopped fresh basil
1 tablespoon chopped fresh parsley
3 tablespoons lemon juice
1 tablespoon capers, drained
1 teaspoon freshly ground pepper
½ teaspoon salt
1 green onion, chopped

Place all ingredients in food processor or blender; cover and process until smooth.

BROILED SEAFOOD KABOBS: Set oven control to broil. Place kabobs on rack in broiler pan. Broil with tops about 4 inches from heat 4 minutes, brushing with Marinade occasionally. Turn kabobs; brush with Marinade. Broil about 4 minutes longer, brushing with Marinade occasionally, until fish flakes easily with fork. Discard bay leaves.

SERVING SIZE: 1 Serving 535 Calories (160 Calories from Fat); Fat 18 g (Saturated 4 g); Cholesterol 430 mg; Sodium 340 mg; Carbohydrate 8 g; (Dietary Fiber 1 g); Protein 86 g; % Daily Value: Vitamin A 24%; Vitamin C 50%; Calcium 10%; Iron 18%

Grilled Shrimp and Scallop Kabobs

¼ cup lemon juice
¼ cup vegetable oil
1 tablespoon chopped fresh or 1 teaspoon dried thyme
¼ teaspoon salt
¼ teaspoon pepper
¾ pound sea scallops
12 raw large shrimp (in shells)
8 medium whole mushrooms (about 6 ounces)
8 cherry tomatoes
1 medium zucchini (about 1 inch in diameter), cut into 1-inch slices

Mix lemon juice, oil, thyme, salt and pepper. Cut scallops in half if over 1 inch in diameter. Arrange scallops, shrimp and vegetables alternately on four 10-inch metal skewers. Brush with lemon-thyme mixture. Grill 4 inches from medium coals 10 to 15 minutes, brushing with mixture frequently, until scallops are opaque in center, and shrimp are pink. **4 servings**

SERVING SIZE: 1 Serving 265 Calories (135 Calories from Fat); Fat 15 g (Saturated 2 g); Cholesterol 65 mg; Sodium 410 mg; Carbohydrate 8 g; (Dietary Fiber 1 g); Protein 25 g; % Daily Value: Vitamin A 8%; Vitamin C 12%; Calcium 12%; Iron 24%

Garlic Shrimp

¹/₂ cup (1 stick) margarine or butter
2 teaspoons garlic salt
¹/₈ teaspoon red pepper sauce
3 pounds cleaned raw shrimp
1 can (8 ounces) sliced water chestnuts, drained
1 large green pepper, cut into rings
1 tablespoon finely chopped onion
¹/₂ teaspoon salt
¹/₂ teaspoon dried tarragon leaves

Form a pan, 11×11×¹/₂ inch, from double thickness heavy-duty aluminum foil. Place margarine, garlic salt and pepper sauce in pan; place on grill 4 to 6 inches from medium coals until margarine is melted. Remove pan from grill; add remaining ingredients. Cover pan with piece of heavy-duty aluminum foil, sealing edges well. Grill until shrimp is done, 20 to 30 minutes.

12 servings

SERVING SIZE: 1 Serving 155 Calories (80 Calories from Fat); Fat 9 g (Saturated 2 g); Cholesterol 160 mg; Sodium 530 mg; Carbohydrate 1 g; (Dietary Fiber 0 g); Protein 17 g; *% Daily Value*: Vitamin A 16%; Vitamin C 8%; Calcium 4%; Iron 14%

Grilled Lobster Tails

The distinctive flavor and texture of lobster make it a favorite of seafood lovers.

6 medium fresh or frozen lobster tails
¹/₂ cup (1 stick) margarine or butter, melted
¹/₃ cup lemon juice
2 teaspoons Worcestershire sauce
¹/₂ teaspoon onion salt
Margarine or butter, melted
Lemon wedges

Thaw lobster tails if frozen; cut away thin undershell (covering meat of lobster tails) with kitchen scissors. To prevent tail from curling, bend each tail backward toward shell; crack. Mix ¹/₂ cup margarine, the lemon juice, Worcestershire sauce and onion salt.

Cover and grill lobster tails, shell sides down, about 4 inches from medium coals 10 minutes, brusing 4 to 6 times with margarine mixture; turn lobster tails. Cover and grill until meat is opaque, 5 to 10 minutes longer. Serve with melted margarine and the lemon wedges.

6 servings

SERVING SIZE: 1 Serving 240 Calories (145 Calories from Fat); Fat 16 g (Saturated 3 g); Cholesterol 75 mg; Sodium 720 mg; Carbohydrate 3 g; (Dietary Fiber 0 g); Protein 21 g *% Daily Value*: Vitamin A 22%; Vitamin C 2%; Calcium 6%; Iron 2%

Grilling Tips

- Whether you use a gas or charcoal grill, be sure to follow the manufacturer's directions for safe use.
- Most fish cooks over medium heat. You'll know your heat is properly adjusted when you can hold your hand, palm down, near but not on the grill for at least two seconds.
- Grilling baskets make turning delicate fish a breeze. If you don't have one, try wiring two wire cooling racks together.
- Long-handled grilling utensils and fire- and heat-resistant mitts do a great job of protecting your hands.
- Keep a spray bottle filled with cold water handy to control fire flare-ups.

Bouillabaisse

Bouillabaisse

Serve lots of crusty French bread to mop up the flavorful broth, or ladle the soup over a thick slice of toasted, crusty bread.

1 cup chopped onion
$1/4$ cup chopped carrot
1 clove garlic, finely chopped
$1/2$ cup vegetable oil
3 pounds frozen fish fillets, thawed and cut into 3-inch pieces
1 can (16 ounces) whole tomatoes, undrained
2 bay leaves
2 quarts water
6 fresh or frozen lobster tails, cut lengthwise into halves
1 pound fresh or frozen shelled raw shrimp
1 can (10 ounces) whole clams, undrained
1 can ($10^1/2$ ounces) beef broth
$1/2$ cup chopped pimiento
$1/4$ cup snipped fresh parsley
1 tablespoon salt
1 tablespoon lemon juice
$1/2$ teaspoon saffron
Dash of pepper

SERVING SIZE: 1 Serving 215 Calories (35 Calories from Fat); Fat 4 g (Saturated 1 g); Cholesterol 65 mg; Sodium 890 mg; Carbohydrate 19 g; (Dietary Fiber 2 g); Protein 24 g; *% Daily Value*: Vitamin A 42%; Vitamin C 28%; Calcium 8%; Iron 56%

Creamy Fish Chowder

This rich-looking chowder is light on calories but full of flavor.

2 cups cubed potatoes (about 2 medium)
1 cup $1/4$-inch slices carrots (about
   2 medium)
$1/2$ cup chopped onion (about 1 medium)
1 cup clam juice
1 cup water
1 tablespoon reduced-calorie margarine
$1/2$ teaspoon salt
$1/4$ teaspoon pepper
1 pound haddock or other lean fish fillets,
   cut into 1-inch pieces
1 can ($6^1/2$ ounces) whole clams, undrained
1 can (12 ounces) evaporated skim milk
2 tablespoons chopped fresh chives
1 teaspoon paprika

Heat potatoes, carrots, onion, clam juice, water, margarine, salt and pepper to boiling in 3-quart saucepan; reduce heat. Cover and simmer 15 to 20 minutes or until potatoes are almost tender.

Stir in fish and clams. Cover and heat to boiling; reduce heat. Simmer about 5 minutes or until fish flakes easily with fork. Stir in milk, chives and paprika; heat through.

8 servings, about 1 cup each

SERVING SIZE: 1 Serving 145 Calories (20 Calories from Fat); Fat 2 g (Saturated 0 g); Cholesterol 40 mg; Sodium 380 mg; Carbohydrate 16 g; (Dietary Fiber 1 g); Protein 17 g; *% Daily Value*: Vitamin A 38%; Vitamin C 12%; Calcium 16%; Iron 20%

Seafood Stew with Rosmarina

Fresh Salmon Chowder

Dill weed complements the salmon in this fresh chowder.

3 slices bacon, chopped
2 medium leeks, thinly sliced
1 clove garlic, crushed
$1/3$ cup chopped fresh or 2 tablespoons
   dried dill weed
$3/4$ teaspoon salt
$1/2$ teaspoon white pepper
2 cups fish stock or clam juice
$1 1/2$ pounds small red potatoes, cut into
   1-inch pieces
1 pound fresh or frozen salmon fillet,
   skinned and cut into 1-inch pieces
4 cups half-and-half
1 cup fresh or frozen whole kernel corn

Cook bacon in large saucepan over medium heat until crisp. Drain fat, reserving 1 tablespoon. Cook leeks and garlic in fat about 5 minutes until leeks are soft. Stir in dill weed, salt, white pepper, fish stock and potatoes.

Cook uncovered over low heat 15 to 20 minutes until potatoes are tender, but not soft. Add remaining ingredients and cook 10 to 15 minutes until salmon is done. **8 servings**

SERVING SIZE: 1 Serving 235 Calories (115 Calories from Fat); Fat 13 g (Saturated 7 g); Cholesterol 55 mg; Sodium 350 mg; Carbohydrate 19 g; (Dietary Fiber 2 g); Protein 13 g; *% Daily Value*: Vitamin A 10%; Vitamin C 8%; Calcium 10%; Iron 6%

New England Clam Chowder

New Englanders claim to have invented chowder, and they're famous for serving up a hearty all-white clam chowder. To finish off this chowder, sprinkle with paprika, fresh chives, parsley, tarragon or dill.

$1/4$ cup cut-up bacon or lean salt pork
$1/2$ cup chopped onion (about 1 medium)
2 cans ($6 1/2$ ounces each) minced clams,
   drained and liquid reserved
2 cups diced potatoes (about 2 medium)
Dash of pepper
2 cups milk

Cook and stir bacon and onion in 2-quart saucepan until bacon is crisp. Add enough water, if necessary, to reserved clam liquid to measure 1 cup. Stir clams, liquid, potatoes and pepper into onion mixture. Heat to boiling; reduce heat. Cover and boil until potatoes are tender, about 15 minutes. Stir in milk. Heat, stirring occasionally, just until hot (do not boil). **4 servings**

SERVING SIZE: 1 Serving 210 Calories (55 Calories from Fat); Fat 6 g (Saturated 3 g); Cholesterol 40 mg; Sodium 190 mg; Carbohydrate 23 g; (Dietary Fiber 1 g); Protein 17 g; *% Daily Value*: Vitamin A 12%; Vitamin C 14%; Calcium 20%; Iron 66%

New England Clam Chowder

Manhattan Clam Chowder

The classic New England Clam Chowder was modified to use tomatoes in place of the cream, and Manhattan Clam Chowder was created.

1/4 cup finely chopped bacon or salt port
1/4 cup finely chopped onion, (about
    1 small)
1 pint shucked fresh clams with liquid*
2 cups finely chopped potatoes
1/3 cup chopped celery
1 cup water
2 teaspoons chopped fresh parsley
1/2 teaspoon salt
1 teaspoon chopped fresh or 1/4 teaspoon
    dried thyme leaves
1/8 teaspoon pepper
1 can (16 ounces) whole tomatoes,
    undrained

Cook bacon and onion in Dutch oven, stirring occasionally, until bacon is crisp and onion is tender. Stir clams and clam liquid, potatoes, celery and water into bacon and onion. Heat to boiling; reduce heat. Cover and simmer about 10 minutes or until potatoes are tender. Stir in remaining ingredients. Break up tomatoes. Heat to boiling, stirring occasionally.

5 servings, about 1 1/4 cups each

2 cans (6 1/2 ounces each) minced clams, undrained, can be substituted for fresh clams. Stir in clams with remaining ingredients.

SERVING SIZE: 1 Serving 165 Calories (25 Calories from Fat); Fat 3 g (Saturated 1 g); Cholesterol 35 mg; Sodium 490 mg; Carbohydrate 21 g; (Dietary Fiber 2 g); Protein 15 g; % *Daily Value*: Vitamin A 14%; Vitamin C 28%; Calcium 8%; Iron 40%

Baja Seafood Stew

1/2 cup chopped onion (about 1 medium)
1/2 cup chopped green chiles
2 cloves garlic, finely chopped
1/4 cup olive oil
2 cups dry white wine
1 tablespoon grated orange peel
1 1/2 cups orange juice
1 tablespoon sugar
1 tablespoon snipped fresh cilantro
1 teaspoon dried basil leaves
1 teaspoon salt
1/2 teaspoon pepper
1/2 teaspoon dried oregano leaves
1 can (28 ounces) whole Italian plum
    tomatoes, undrained and cut into
    halves
24 soft-shell clams (steamers), scrubbed
1 1/2 pounds shelled medium raw shrimp
1 pound cod, sea bass, mahimahi or red
    snapper fillets, cut into 1-inch pieces
1 package (6 ounces) frozen crabmeat,
    thawed, drained and cartilage removed

Cook and stir onion, chiles and garlic in oil in 6-quart Dutch oven until onion is tender. Stir in remaining ingredients except the seafood. Heat to boiling; reduce heat. Simmer uncovered 15 minutes.

Add clams; cover and simmer until clams open, 5 to 10 minutes. (Discard any clams that do not open.) Carefully stir in shrimp, cod and crabmeat. Heat to boiling; reduce heat. Cover and simmer until shrimp are pink and cod flakes easily with fork, 4 to 5 minutes.

6 to 8 servings, about 1 1/2 cups each

SERVING SIZE: 1 Serving 400 Calories (110 Calories from Fat); Fat 12 g (Saturated 2 g); Cholesterol 245 mg; Sodium 1060 mg; Carbohydrate 20 g; (Dietary Fiber 2 g); Protein 45 g; % *Daily Value*: Vitamin A 18%; Vitamin C 52%; Calcium 14%; Iron 64%

Oyster and Vegetable Chowder

$^1/_3$ cup margarine or butter
1$^1/_2$ pints shucked select or large oysters, undrained*
1 package (16 ounces) frozen corn-broccoli mixture
3$^1/_2$ cups milk
1$^1/_2$ teaspoons salt
Dash of pepper

Heat margarine in 3-quart saucepan until melted. Stir in oysters and vegetables. Cook over medium heat, stirring frequently, until edges of oysters are curled and vegetables are done, about 14 minutes.

Stir in milk, salt and pepper. Cook over low heat, stirring frequently, until hot.   **6 servings**

*3 cans (8 ounces each) whole oysters, undrained, can be substituted for fresh oysters; stir in with the milk.

SERVING SIZE: 1 Serving 285 Calories (145 Calories from Fat); Fat 16 g (Saturated 5 g); Cholesterol 75 mg; Sodium 990 mg; Carbohydrate 21 g; (Dietary Fiber 2 g); Protein 16 g; % Daily Value: Vitamin A 32%; Vitamin C 16%; Calcium 24%; Iron 48%

Crab Bisque

1 teaspoon grated onion
1 tablespoon margarine or butter
1 tablespoon all-purpose flour
2 teaspoons snipped parsley
1 teaspoon salt
$^1/_8$ teaspoon pepper
$^1/_8$ teaspoon celery salt
2 cups milk
1 cup water or chicken broth
1 can (7$^1/_2$ ounces) crabmeat, chopped, with crabmeat liquid

Cook and stir onion in margarine over low heat. Stir in flour, parsley, salt, pepper and celery salt. Cook, stirring constantly, until mixture is smooth and bubbly. Remove from heat; stir in milk and water. Heat to boiling, stirring constantly. Boil and stir 1 minute. Stir in crab (with liquid).

          4 servings

SERVING SIZE: 1 Serving 200 Calories (45 Calories from Fat); Fat 5 g (Saturated 2 g); Cholesterol 40 mg; Sodium 1070 mg; Carbohydrate 26 g; (Dietary Fiber 2 g); Protein 15 g; % Daily Value: Vitamin A 10%; Vitamin C 28%; Calcium 16%; Iron 12%

Lobster Bisque

$^1/_4$ cup finely chopped onion (about 1 small)
3 tablespoons margarine or butter
3 tablespoons all-purpose flour
1 tablespoon snipped fresh parsley
$^1/_2$ teaspoon salt
$^1/_8$ teaspoon pepper
2 cups milk
1 cup water or chicken broth
1$^1/_4$ cups chopped fresh or frozen (thawed) lobster (about 12 ounces)

Cook and stir onion in butter in 3-quart saucepan over low heat until onion is tender. Stir in flour, parsley, salt and pepper. Cook stirring constantly, until mixture is bubbly; remove from heat. Stir in milk and water. Heat to boiling, stirring constantly. Boil and stir 1 minute. Stir in lobster. Heat to boiling; reduce heat. Cook about 3 minutes, stirring frequently, until lobster is white.   **4 servings, about 1 cup each**

SERVING SIZE: 1 Serving 205 Calories (100 Calories from Fat); Fat 11 g (Saturated 7 g); Cholesterol 65 mg; Sodium 560 mg; Carbohydrate 13 g; (Dietary Fiber 0 g); Protein 14 g; % Daily Value: Vitamin A 14%; Vitamin C 2%; Calcium 18%; Iron 4%

Shrimp Gumbo

Creole cooks in Louisiana devised the gumbo, a hearty soup traditionally thickened with either okra or filé powder. Filé powder, made from dried, pulverized sassafras leaves, must be added at the very end of the cooking time; otherwise it becomes stringy.

2 cloves garlic, finely chopped
2 medium onions, sliced
$1/2$ medium green bell pepper, thinly sliced
2 tablespoons margarine or butter
12 ounces fresh okra, cut into $1/2$-inch pieces*
1 can (16 ounces) tomatoes, undrained
1 can (6 ounces) tomato paste
3 cups beef broth
1 tablespoon Worcestershire sauce
1 teaspoon salt
1 teaspoon chile powder
1 teaspoon snipped fresh or $1/2$ teaspoon dried basil
$1/4$ teaspoon pepper
1 bay leaf
$1^{1}/2$ pounds cleaned raw shrimp**
1 tablespoon filé powder
3 cups hot cooked rice

Cook and stir garlic, onions and bell pepper in butter in Dutch oven over medium heat until tender. Stir in okra, tomatoes, tomato paste, broth, Worcestershire sauce, salt, chile powder, basil, pepper and bay leaf. Break up tomatoes with fork. Heat to boiling; reduce heat. Simmer uncovered 45 minutes. Stir in shrimp. Cover and simmer 5 minutes or until shrimp are pink and tender. Remove bay leaf; stir in filé powder. Serve with hot cooked rice.

8 servings, about 1 cup each

*1 package (10 ounces) frozen okra can be substituted for the fresh okra.
**About $1^{1}/2$ pounds fresh or frozen raw shrimp in shells.

SERVING SIZE: 1 Serving 220 Calories (35 Calories from Fat); Fat 4 g (Saturated 2 g); Cholesterol 130 mg; Sodium 950 mg; Carbohydrate 31 g; (Dietary Fiber 4 g); Protein 19 g; *% Daily Value*: Vitamin A 18%; Vitamin C 24%; Calcium 10%; Iron 24%

Scallop and Shrimp Minestrone

2 cups chopped onions (about 2 large)
$1/2$ cup chopped carrot (about 1 medium)
1 cup chicken broth
1 clove garlic, finely chopped
$1^{1}/2$ cups tomato juice
2 tablespoons lemon juice
1 can ($14^{1}/2$ ounces) whole tomatos, cut and undrained
1 bay leaf
$1/2$ cup uncooked medium pasta shells | rice
$1/2$ cup chopped mushrooms (about 4 ounces)
$1/2$ cup chopped yellow summer squash
$1/2$ cup chopped zucchini
2 tablespoons chopped fresh parsley
$1/4$ teaspoon salt
12 raw large shrimp, peeled and deveined
6 ounces sea scallops

Cook onions, carrots, broth and garlic in 2-quart saucepan over medium heat 5 minutes, stirring occasionally. Stir in tomato juice, lemon juice, tomatoes and bay leaf. Reduce heat. Simmer covered 10 minutes.

Stir in pasta. Cook 7 minutes. Stir in remaining ingredients. Cover and cook 5 minutes, stirring occasionally, until shrimp are pink. **6 servings**

SERVING SIZE: 1 Serving 145 Calories (10 Calories from Fat); Fat 1 g (Saturated 0 g); Cholesterol 35 mg; Sodium 660 mg; Carbohydrate 23 g; (Dietary Fiber 3 g); Protein 14 g; *% Daily Value*: Vitamin A 30%; Vitamin C 26%; Calcium 8%; Iron 16%

Shrimp Gumbo

Cajun Seafood and Noodles (page 74)

5

Seafood and Pasta

Salmon with Cucumber Sauce

1/2 **pound salmon fillets* or other fatty fish**
1 cup plain nonfat yogurt
1 tablespoon all-purpose flour
1 tablespoon chopped fresh or
   1 teaspoon dried dill weed
1 teaspoon prepared horseradish
1 cup chopped seeded unpeeled
   cucumber (about 1 medium)
1 cup uncooked medium shell (conchiglie)
   or seashell macaroni (about 4 ounces)

Place salmon fillets in 2-quart saucepan; add enough water to cover. Heat to boiling; reduce heat. Simmer uncovered 6 to 8 minutes or until fish flakes easily with fork. Remove fish with slotted spatula; drain. Remove any skin. Flake fish into bite-size pieces; keep warm.

Mix yogurt and flour in same 2-quart saucepan. Stir in dill weed and horseradish. Heat over low heat until hot (do not boil). Stir in cucumber and fish. Cook macaroni as directed on package; drain. Serve sauce over macaroni. Garnish with thinly sliced cucumber, if desired.

4 servings, about 1 cup each

*1 can (6³/₄ ounces) skinless boneless pink salmon, drained and flaked, can be substituted for the salmon fillets. Do not cook.

SERVING SIZE: 1 Serving 235 Calories (35 Calories from Fat); Fat 4 g (Saturated 1 g); Cholesterol 35 mg; Sodium 75 mg; Carbohydrate 32 g; (Dietary Fiber 1 g); Protein 19 g; *% Daily Value*: Vitamin A *%; Vitamin C *%; Calcium 14%; Iron 11%

Lemon Seafood with Pasta

Microwaving makes this a no-fuss and delicious dinner.

1/2 **pound fresh or frozen (thawed) raw medium shrimp, peeled and deveined**
1/2 **pound bay scallops**
1 **medium zucchini, cut into 1/4-inch slices (about 1 1/2 cups)**
1 **medium yellow squash, cut into 1/4-inch slices (about 1 1/2 cups)**
1 **small yellow or green bell pepper, cut into 1/4-inch strips**
1 **cup chicken broth**
1/4 **cup lemon juice**
2 **tablespoons cornstarch**
1 **tablespoon chopped fresh or 1 teaspoon dried dill weed**
1/4 **teaspoon salt**
2 **cups hot cooked rotini pasta**

Mix shrimp, scallops, zucchini, squash and bell pepper in 3-quart microwavable casserole. Cover casserole tightly and microwave on high 8 to 10 minutes, stirring every 3 minutes, until shrimp are pink; drain. Let stand covered 5 minutes.

Mix broth, lemon juice, cornstarch, dill weed and salt in 2-cup microwavable measure until smooth. Microwave uncovered on high 3 to 4 minutes, stirring every minute, until mixture thickens and boils. Stir into seafood mixture. Serve over pasta. Garnish with fresh dill weed, if desired.   **4 servings**

SERVING SIZE: 1 Serving 240 Calories (20 Calories from Fat); Fat 2 g (Saturated 0 g); Cholesterol 100 mg; Sodium 580 mg; Carbohydrate 30 g; (Dietary Fiber 2 g); Protein 27 g; % *Daily Value*: Vitamin A 8%; Vitamin C 20%; Calcium 10%; Iron 26%

Cajun Seafood and Noodles

If frozen shrimp and crab are not readily available, canned shrimp and crab are just as delicious.

3 **cups uncooked medium noodles (about 6 ounces)**
1 **tablespoon vegetable oil**
3/4 **cup chopped green bell pepper (about 1 medium)**
1/2 **cup chopped onion (about 1 medium)**
2 **tablespoons chopped fresh parsley**
1/8 **teaspoon ground red pepper (cayenne)**
1/8 **teaspoon pepper**
2 **cloves garlic, finely chopped**
1 **tablespoon all-purpose flour**
1 **can (16 ounces) whole tomatoes, undrained**
1 **package (10 ounces) frozen cut okra, thawed**
1 **package (6 ounces) frozen cooked small shrimp, thawed and drained**
1 **package (6 ounces) frozen crabmeat, thawed, drained and cartilage removed**

Cook noodles as directed on package; drain. Heat oil in 10-inch nonstick skillet over medium heat. Cook bell pepper, onion, parsley, red pepper, pepper, and garlic 3 minutes, stirring frequently. Stir in flour and tomatoes; break up tomatoes.

Cook uncovered, stirring frequently, until mixture thickens and boils. Stir in okra, shrimp and crabmeat. Cook uncovered 5 minutes, stirring occasionally. Serve over noodles.

6 servings, about 2/3 cup fish mixture and 1/2 cup noodles each

SERVING SIZE: 1 Serving 190 Calories (35 Calories from Fat); Fat 4 g (Saturated 1 g); Cholesterol 90 mg; Sodium 250 mg; Carbohydrate 28 g; (Dietary Fiber 4 g); Protein 15 g; % *Daily Value*: Vitamin A 10%; Vitamin C 26%; Calcium 10%; Iron 16%

Lemon Seafood with Pasta

Seafood Marinara with Linguine

8 ounces uncooked linguine
$3/4$ cup tomato puree
$3/4$ cup white wine or apple juice
2 cloves garlic, finely chopped
1 teaspoon olive or vegetable oil
1 can ($14^1/2$ ounces) whole tomatoes, undrained
1-pound yellowfin tuna or other lean fish fillet, cut into 1-inch pieces
3 tablespoons chopped fresh or 1 tablespoon dried basil leaves
1 teaspoon grated lemon peel
2 tablespoons lemon juice
2 teaspoons capers
$1/4$ teaspoon pepper

Cook pasta according to package directions—except omit salt; drain. Cook tomato puree, wine, garlic, oil and tomatoes in 2-quart saucepan over medium heat 10 minutes, breaking up tomatoes and stirring occasionally. Stir in fish. Cover and simmer 7 minutes or until fish flakes easily with fork. Stir in cooked linguine and remaining ingredients.   **6 servings**

SERVING SIZE: 1 Serving 265 Calories (25 Calories from Fat); Fat 3 g (Saturated 0 g); Cholesterol 40 mg; Sodium 310 mg; Carbohydrate 37 g; (Dietary Fiber 2 g); Protein 21 g; *% Daily Value*: Vitamin A 10%; Vitamin C 14%; Calcium 4%; Iron 14%

Clam Linguine

3 quarts water
1 teaspoon salt
2 cans ($6^1/2$ ounces each) minced clams, drained (reserve liquid)
1 package (8 ounces) linguine or spaghetti
$1/4$ cup ($1/2$ stick) margarine or butter
2 tablespoons snipped parsley
1 tablespoon snipped fresh basil leaves or $1^1/2$ teaspoons dried basil leaves
$3/4$ teaspoon snipped fresh thyme leaves or $1/4$ teaspoon dried thyme leaves
Dash of pepper
3 cloves garlic, finely chopped
$1/2$ cup whipping cream
$1/4$ cup Emerald Riesling or dry white wine
$1/4$ cup grated Parmesan cheese

Heat water, salt and reserved clam liquid to boiling in 4-quart Dutch oven. Gradually add linguine. Boil uncovered, stirring occasionally, just until tender, 8 to 10 minutes; drain. Return to Dutch oven; toss with 2 tablespoons of the margarine.

Heat remaining 2 tablespoons margarine in 2-quart saucepan. Stir in parsley, basil, thyme, pepper, garlic and clams. Cook over low heat, stirring constantly, until clams are heated through. Stir in whipping cream and wine; heat through, stirring occasionally. Pour over linguine; add Parmesan cheese. Toss until evenly coated.   **4 servings**

SERVING SIZE: 1 Serving 490 Calories (215 Calories from Fat); Fat 24 g (Saturated 9 g); Cholesterol 65 mg; Sodium 510 mg; Carbohydrate 50 g; (Dietary Fiber 2 g); Protein 21 g; *% Daily Value*: Vitamin A 30%; Vitamin C 10%; Calcium 16%; Iron 40%

Clam Linguine

Mixed Herb Spaghetti and Clam Sauce

Tomatoes and herbs give this clam sauce a very Italian taste.

2 cups chopped tomatoes (about 2 large)

1 cup tomato juice

¹/₂ cup dry white wine or tomato juice

2 tablespoons lemon juice

1 teaspoon olive or vegetable oil

¹/₄ teaspoon salt

¹/₄ teaspoon pepper

¹/₄ cup chopped fresh parsley

2 tablespoons chopped fresh or
2 teaspoons dried basil leaves

2 cans (10 ounces each) whole baby
clams, drained

6 cups hot cooked spaghetti

Heat tomatoes, tomato juice, wine, lemon juice, oil, salt and pepper to boiling in Dutch oven; reduce heat. Simmer uncovered 5 minutes or until slightly thickened. Stir in parsley, basil and clams. Serve over spaghetti. **6 servings**

SERVING SIZE: 1 Serving 335 Calories (25 Calories from Fat); Fat 3 g (Saturated 0 g); Cholesterol 50 mg; Sodium 330 mg; Carbohydrate 49 g; (Dietary Fiber 2 g); Protein 27 g; *% Daily Value*: Vitamin A 20%; Vitamin C 32%; Calcium 8%; Iron 100%

Microwaving Fish

Arrange fish fillets or steaks, thickest parts to outside edges, in shallow microwavable dish large enough to hold pieces in single layer. Cover tightly and microwave on high as directed below or until fish flakes easily with fork.

Fish	Amount	Time	Stand Time
Fillets, ¹/₂ to ³/₄ inch thick	1 pound rotating dish ¹/₂ turn after 3 minutes	5 to 7 minutes,	2 minutes
	1¹/₂ pounds rotating dish ¹/₂ turn after 4 minutes	7 to 9 minutes,	3 minutes
Steaks, 1-inch thick	1 pound ¹/₂ turn after 3 minutes	5 to 7 minutes, rotating dish	3 minutes
	2 pounds rotating dish ¹/₂ turn after 4 minutes	8 to 10 minutes,	3 minutes

Marinated Tuna with Pasta

2 cans (6½ ounces each) tuna in water, drained
1½ cups chopped tomatoes (about 2 medium)
1 small onion, thinly sliced and separated into rings
½ cup pitted small ripe olives
2 cloves garlic, crushed
2 tablespoons olive or vegetable oil
2 tablespoons snipped parsley
½ teaspoon salt
½ teaspoon dried basil leaves
¼ teaspoon dried oregano leaves
⅛ teaspoon coarsely ground pepper
2 cups uncooked pasta bows (farfalle)

Mix all ingredients except pasta bows. Cover and refrigerate at least 2 hours but no longer than 24 hours.

Cook bows as directed on package; drain. Immediately toss with tuna mixture. Serve on lettuce and garnish with anchovies, if desired.

5 servings, about 1 cup each

SERVING SIZE: 1 Serving 350 Calories (80 Calories from Fat); Fat 9 g (Saturated 1 g); Cholesterol 20 mg; Sodium 560 mg; Carbohydrate 45 g; (Dietary Fiber 2 g); Protein 24 g; *% Daily Value*: Vitamin A 6%; Vitamin C 10%; Calcium 4%; Iron 22%

Creamy Tuna Casserole

An all-time favorite!

8 ounces uncooked noodles
1 can (12½ ounces) tuna, drained
1 can (4 ounces) sliced mushrooms, drained
1 jar (2 ounces) sliced pimientos, drained
1½ cups sour cream
¾ cup milk
¼ teaspoon pepper
¼ cup dry bread crumbs
¼ cup grated Parmesan cheese
2 tablespoons margarine or butter, melted
Chopped fresh parsley

Heat oven to 350°. Cook noodles as directed on package; drain. Mix noodles, tuna, mushrooms, pimientos, sour cream, milk and pepper in ungreased 2-quart casserole. Mix bread crumbs, cheese and margarine. Sprinkle over tuna mixture.

Bake uncovered 35 to 40 minutes or until hot and bubbly. Sprinkle with parsley.   **6 servings**

SERVING SIZE: 1 Serving 430 Calories (205 Calories from Fat); Fat 23 g (Saturated 10 g); Cholesterol 85 mg; Sodium 450 mg; Carbohydrate 33 g; (Dietary Fiber 2 g); Protein 25 g; *% Daily Value*: Vitamin A 20%; Vitamin C 6%; Calcium 16%; Iron 16%

Creamy Italian Shrimp

Southwest Scallops

Can't find Anaheim chiles? Use a small red bell pepper. It gives the sauce a milder and sweeter flavor.

1 red Anaheim chile, chopped
$1/4$ cup sliced green onions
     (about 3 medium)
2 tablespoons reduced-calorie margarine
2 tablespoons lime juice
2 pounds sea scallops
2 cups cubed fresh pineapple
1 cup Chinese pea pod halves
     (about 3 ounces)
3 cups hot cooked fettuccine

Cook chile, onions, margarine and lime juice in 10-inch nonstick skillet, stirring occasionally, until margarine is melted. Carefully stir in scallops. Cook over medium heat about 12 minutes, stirring frequently, until scallops are white. Stir in pineapple and pea pods. Heat until hot. Remove scallop mixture with slotted spoon; keep warm.

Heat liquid in skillet to boiling. Boil until slightly thickened and reduced to about half. Spoon scallop mixture onto fettuccine; pour liquid over scallop mixture.

6 servings, about $1^1/2$ cups each

SERVING SIZE: 1 Serving 320 Calories (45 Calories from Fat); Fat 5 g (Saturated 1 g); Cholesterol 75 mg; Sodium 460 mg; Carbohydrate 33 g; (Dietary Fiber 2 g); Protein 38 g; *% Daily Value*: Vitamin A 20%; Vitamin C 26%; Calcium 20%; Iron 36%

Creamy Italian Shrimp

1 pound fresh or frozen raw medium
     shrimp (in shells)
6 ounces uncooked linguine or fettuccine,
     broken into 3-inch pieces
1 tablespoon olive or vegetable oil
1 to 2 cloves garlic, finely chopped
1 tablespoon olive or vegetable oil
2 small zucchini, cut lengthwise in half
     and thinly sliced (about 2 cups)
1 cup half-and-half
$3/4$ cup grated Parmesan cheese
$1/4$ cup pesto
1 tablespoon chopped fresh or 1 teaspoon
     dried rosemary leaves
2 teaspoons lemon juice
$1/4$ teaspoon pepper
2 medium tomatoes, seeded and cut into
     bite-size pieces

Peel shrimp. (If shrimp are frozen, do not thaw; peel in cold water.) Make a shallow cut lengthwise down the back of each shrimp; wash out vein. Cook linguine as directed on package; drain. Rinse in cold water; drain.

Heat wok or 12-inch skillet until very hot. Add 1 tablespoon oil to wok; rotate wok to coat sides. Add shrimp and garlic; stir-fry about 3 minutes or until shrimp are pink. Remove shrimp mixture from wok.

Add 1 tablespoon oil to wok; rotate wok to coat sides. Add zucchini; stir-fry about 3 minutes or until crisp-tender. Stir in half-and-half, cheese, pesto, rosemary, lemon juice and pepper. Cook and stir 1 to 2 minutes or until slightly thickened. Stir in shrimp mixture, linguine and tomatoes. Cook about 1 minute or until heated through.

4 servings

SERVING SIZE: 1 Serving 535 Calories (260 Calories from Fat); Fat 29 g (Saturated 11 g); Cholesterol 145 mg; Sodium 490 mg; Carbohydrate 43 g; (Dietary Fiber 3 g); Protein 28 g; *% Daily Value*: Vitamin A 18%; Vitamin C 16%; Calcium 36%; Iron 24%

Scallops Tetrazzini

**6 ounces uncooked spaghetti, broken into
3-inch pieces
1 pound bay or sea scallops
1¹/₂ cups water
1 tablespoon lemon juice
3 tablespoons margarine or butter
2 cups sliced mushrooms
¹/₂ cup sliced green onions
(about 5 medium)
3 tablespoons all-purpose flour
³/₄ teaspoon ground mustard
¹/₄ teaspoon salt
¹/₄ teaspoon pepper
¹/₄ teaspoon paprika
2 cups milk
¹/₄ cup grated Romano cheese
2 tablespoons dry sherry, if desired
¹/₄ cup grated Romano cheese**

Heat oven to 350°. Cook spaghetti as directed on package; drain. Meanwhile, cut sea scallops into fourths. Mix scallops, water and lemon juice in 1¹/₂-quart saucepan. Heat to boiling; reduce heat. Simmer uncovered 1 to 3 minutes or until scallops are white. Remove scallops from saucepan; reserve ¹/₂ cup liquid.

Heat margarine in same saucepan over medium heat until melted. Cook mushrooms and onions in margarine about 3 minutes, stirring frequently, until vegetables are crisp-tender. Stir in flour, mustard, salt, pepper and paprika. Cook over medium heat, stirring constantly, until bubbly; remove from heat. Stir in milk and reserved liquid. Heat to boiling, stirring constantly. Boil and stir 1 minute. Stir in ¹/₄ cup cheese and the sherry.

Mix cooked spaghetti, scallops and sauce in ungreased rectangular pan, 11 × 7 × 1¹/₂ inches. Sprinkle with ¹/₄ cup cheese. Bake uncovered 25 to 30 minutes or until heated through.

4 servings

SERVING SIZE: 1 Serving 515 Calories (155 Calories from Fat); Fat 17 g (Saturated 6 g); Cholesterol 55 mg; Sodium 790 mg; Carbohydrate 51 g; (Dietary Fiber 2 g); Protein 41 g; % *Daily Value*: Vitamin A 26%; Vitamin C 4%; Calcium 44%; Iron 34%

Creamy Scallops and Pasta

This sauce is deliciously creamy, and it's still healthy!

**¹/₄ cup chopped shallots (about 2 large)
1 can (14 ¹/₂ ounces) chicken broth
1 ¹/₂ teaspoon chopped fresh or ¹/₂ teaspoon dried thyme leaves
¹/₄ cup all-purpose flour
1 ¹/₂ cup low-fat milk
¹/₄ cup non-fat sour cream
¹/₄ teaspoon pepper
¹/₈ teaspoon ground nutmeg
1 pound bay scallops
4 cups hot cooked medium pasta shells (8 ounces)
1 tablespoon chopped fresh parsley
1 teaspoon grated lemon peel**

Cook shallots, broth and thyme in 12-inch skillet over medium heat about 5 minutes or until shallots are tender. Mix flour with ¹/₂ cup milk. Stir flour mixture into broth. Add remaining milk, the sour cream, pepper and nutmeg. Cook 3 to 5 minutes, stirring frequently, until slightly thickened. Stir in scallops and pasta. Cook 2 minutes longer or until scallops are white. Stir in parsley and lemon peel.

6 servings.

Serving Size: 1 Serving 290 Calories (35 Calories from Fat):Fat 4 g (Saturated 2); Cholesterol 30 mg; Sodium 460 mg; Carbohydrate 38g; (Dietary Fiber 1 g); Protein 26g; % *Daily Value*: Vitamin A 18%; Vitamin C 2%; Calcium 18%; Iron 22%

Artichokes and Shrimp with Fettuccine

8 oz. uncooked fettuccine
1 cup plain yogurt
1 tablespoon chopped fresh or 1 teaspoon
    freeze-dried chives
1 teaspoon finely shredded lemon peel
1/2 teaspoon salt
3/4 pound cooked shrimp or 1 package
    (12 ounces) frozen cooked shrimp,
    thawed
1 jar (6 ounces) marinated artichoke
    hearts, undrained
1 package (3 ounces) cream cheese
1 tablespoon chopped fresh or 1 teaspoon
    freeze-dried chives

Cook pasta as directed on package; drain. Mix yogurt, 1 tablespoon chives, the lemon peel, salt, shrimp, artichoke hearts and cream cheese in 2-quart saucepan. Cook over low heat, stirring constantly, until hot and cream cheese is melted. Toss with pasta. Sprinkle with 1 tablespoon chives. **4 servings**

SERVING SIZE: 1 Serving 404 Calories (110 Calories from Fat); Fat 12 g (Saturated 6 g); Cholesterol 240 mg; Sodium 680 mg; Carbohydrate 46 g; (Dietary Fiber 3 g); Protein 31 g; *% Daily Value*: Vitamin A 14%; Vitamin C 6%; Calcium 20%; Iron 32%

Scampi with Fettuccine

1 1/2 pounds fresh or frozen raw medium
    shrimp (in shells)
6 ounces uncooked spinach fettuccine
2 tablespoons olive or vegetable oil
2 tablespoons thinly sliced green onions
1 tablespoon chopped fresh or
    1 1/2 teaspoons dried basil leaves
1 tablespoon chopped fresh parsley
2 tablespoons lemon juice
2 cloves garlic, finely chopped
1/4 teaspoon salt

Peel shrimp. (If shrimp are frozen, do not thaw; peel in cold water.) Make a shallow cut lengthwise down back of each shrimp; wash out vein. Cook fettuccine as directed on package; drain.

Heat oil in 10-inch skillet over medium heat. Stir in shrimp and remaining ingredients. Cook, stirring frequently, 2 to 3 minutes or until shrimp are pink; remove from heat. Toss fettuccine with shrimp mixture in skillet.

4 servings, about 1 cup each

SERVING SIZE: 1 Serving 285 Calories (80 Calories from Fat); Fat 9 g (Saturated 2 g); Cholesterol 200 mg; Sodium 330 mg; Carbohydrate 30 g; (Dietary Fiber 2 g); Protein 23 g; *% Daily Value*: Vitamin A 6%; Vitamin C 4%; Calcium 4%; Iron 26

Deveining Shrimp

Using a small, pointed knife make a shallow cut along the outside length of the shrimp. Remove black vein; wash.

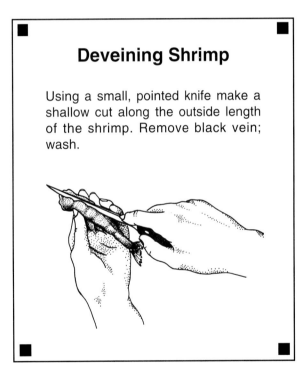

Tarragon-Seafood Salad

6
Seafood Salads

Tarragon-Seafood Salad

3 cups uncooked bow-shaped macaroni
   (about 6 ounces)
4 ounces pea pods, cut into halves
2 tablespoons olive or vegetable oil
1 tablespoon chopped fresh or 1 teaspoon
   dried tarragon
1/2 teaspoon salt
1/4 teaspoon white pepper
2 cloves garlic, finely chopped
3/4 pound seafood sticks, cut into 1/2-inch
   pieces

Cook macaroni as directed on package—except
add pea pods 1 minute before pasta is done;
drain. Rinse pasta and pea pods in cold water;
drain. Gently toss all ingredients.   **4 servings**

SERVING SIZE: 1 Serving 510 Calories (80 Calories from
Fat); Fat 9 g (Saturated 1 g); Cholesterol 25 mg; Sodium
1010 mg; Carbohydrate 84 g; (Dietary Fiber 3 g); Protein
26 g; *% Daily Value*: Vitamin A 2%; Vitamin C 10%; Calcium
4%; Iron 24%

Seafood-Pesto Salad

*You can prepare this enticing salad in
almost no time!*

2 cups uncooked medium shell macaroni
   (about 5 ounces)
2/3 cup pesto
3 Italian pear-shaped tomatoes, cut into
   eighths
1/3 cup small pitted ripe olives
2 tablespoons white wine vinegar
4 ounces spinach, coarsely chopped
   (about 3 cups)
1 1/2 cups bite-size pieces cooked seafood
   (scallops, lobster, shrimp, crab)

Cook macaroni as directed on package; drain.
Rinse in cold water; drain. Mix macaroni, pesto,
tomatoes, olives and vinegar in large bowl. Add
spinach and seafood. Toss.   **4 servings**

SERVING SIZE: 1 Serving 585 Calories (260 Calories from
Fat); Fat 29 g (Saturated 5 g); Cholesterol 55 mg; Sodium
440 mg; Carbohydrate 60 g; (Dietary Fiber 4 g); Protein
25 g; *% Daily Value*: Vitamin A 44%; Vitamin C 22%;
Calcium 26%; Iron 36%

Spicy Seafood Salad

1 cup uncooked regular long grain rice
$\frac{1}{2}$ cup spicy 8-vegetable juice
$\frac{1}{2}$ teaspoon salt
1 cup chopped celery (about 2 medium stalks)
$1\frac{1}{2}$ cups chopped tomatoes (about 2 medium)
1 cup chopped red bell pepper (about 1 medium)
1 package (8 ounces) frozen salad-style imitation crabmeat, thawed
1 package (8 ounces) frozen cooked shrimp, thawed

Cook rice as directed on package. Mix rice and remaining ingredients in large serving bowl. Cover and refrigerate about 1 hour or until chilled. **4 servings**

SERVING SIZE: 1 Serving 285 Calories (20 Calories from Fat); Fat 2 g (Saturated 0 g); Cholesterol 100 mg; Sodium 980 mg; Carbohydrate 47 g; (Dietary Fiber 2 g); Protein 22 g; % *Daily Value*: Vitamin A 22%; Vitamin C 48%; Calcium 4%; Iron 20%

Hot Perch Salad

Use any combination of greens for this salad: Romaine, iceberg, Bibb, spinach or watercress.

2 tablespoons sliced almonds
1 tablespoon thinly sliced green onion
$\frac{1}{4}$ teaspoon salt
$\frac{1}{8}$ teaspoon coarsely ground pepper
1 tablespoon margarine or butter
$\frac{1}{2}$ cup orange juice
1 teaspoon cornstarch
1 pound ocean perch fillets
4 cups bite-size pieces salad greens
2 medium oranges, peeled and sectioned

Cook almonds, onion, salt and pepper in margarine in $1\frac{1}{2}$-quart saucepan about 4 minutes, stirring frequently, until almonds are light brown. Mix orange juice and cornstarch; stir into almond mixture. Cook about 30 seconds, stirring constantly, until thickened.

Set oven control to broil. Cut fish fillets into 4 serving pieces. Place on rack in broiler pan. Broil with tops about 4 inches from heat 5 to 6 minutes or until fish flakes easily with fork (do not turn). Arrange salad greens and orange sections on 4 salad plates. Top with fish. Spoon almond mixture over fish. **4 servings**

TO MICROWAVE: Decrease orange juice to $\frac{1}{3}$ cup. Mix almonds, onion, salt, pepper and margarine in 2-cup microwavable measure. Microwave uncovered on high 2 to 3 minutes, stirring every minute, until almonds are light brown. Mix orange juice and cornstarch; stir into almond mixture. Microwave uncovered on high 30 to 60 seconds or until thickened. Cut fish fillets into 4 serving pieces. Arrange fish, thickest parts to outside edges, in rectangular microwavable dish, $12\times7\frac{1}{2}\times2$ inches. Cover tightly and microwave on high 5 to 7 minutes, rotating dish $\frac{1}{2}$ turn after 3 minutes, until fish flakes easily with fork. Let stand covered 3 minutes. Continue as directed.

SERVING SIZE: 1 Serving 195 Calories (55 Calories from Fat); Fat 6 g (Saturated 1 g); Cholesterol 60 mg; Sodium 270 mg; Carbohydrate 14 g; (Dietary Fiber 2 g); Protein 23 g; % *Daily Value*: Vitamin A 8%; Vitamin C 40%; Calcium 6%; Iron 4%

SEAFOOD SALADS ■ 87

Italian Tuna and Spiral Pasta Salad

If you like, substitute other types of short cut pasta for the macaroni, such as fusilli or farfalle (bow ties).

1 package (7 ounces) uncooked spiral macaroni (about 3 cups)
2 cans (6½ ounces each) tuna, chilled and drained
1 jar (6 ounces) marinated artichoke hearts, chilled and undrained
¼ cup Italian dressing
2 tablespoons snipped parsley
2 tablespoons capers, drained
Dash of pepper

Cook macaroni as directed on package; drain. Rinse in cold water; drain. Mix macaroni and remaining ingredients. Serve on salad greens, if desired. **4 servings**

SERVING SIZE: 1 Serving 375 Calories (90 Calories from Fat); Fat 10 g (Saturated 2 g); Cholesterol 25 mg; Sodium 500 mg; Carbohydrate 44 g; (Dietary Fiber 2 g); Protein 29 g; *% Daily Value*: Vitamin A 2%; Vitamin C 10%; Calcium 4%; Iron 20%

Broiled Tuna-Tomato Salad

What a terrific way to use garden-fresh tomatoes!

2 large tomatoes, each cut into 6 slices
¾ cup blue cheese dressing
¼ cup sliced green onions
2 cans (6½ ounces each) tuna, drained
4 cups bite-size pieces salad greens
3 hard-cooked eggs, cut lengthwise into fourths
4 slices bacon, crisply cooked and crumbled

Set oven control to broil. Place tomato slices on ungreased cookie sheet. Mix dressing, onions and tuna; spread over tomatoes. Broil with tops 2 to 3 inches from heat about 3 minutes or until tuna mixture bubbles.

Divide salad greens among 4 plates. Top with tomato slices, eggs and bacon. **4 servings**

SERVING SIZE: 1 Serving 450 Calories (290 Calories from Fat); Fat 32 g (Saturated 7 g); Cholesterol 195 mg; Sodium 940 mg; Carbohydrate 10 g; (Dietary Fiber 1 g); Protein 31 g; *% Daily Value*: Vitamin A 16%; Vitamin C 20%; Calcium 8%; Iron 14%

Dilled Pasta Salad with Smoked Fish

2 cups uncooked rotini or spiral macaroni
$\frac{1}{2}$ cup mayonnaise or salad dressing
$\frac{1}{4}$ cup plain yogurt or sour cream
1 tablespoon chopped fresh or
    $\frac{1}{2}$ teaspoon dried dill weed
$\frac{1}{2}$ teaspoon dry mustard
$\frac{1}{4}$ teaspoon salt
$\frac{1}{4}$ teaspoon pepper
1 can ($2\frac{1}{4}$ ounces) sliced pitted ripe olives,
    drained (about $\frac{1}{2}$ cup)
2 green onions, thinly sliced
2 cups thinly sliced zucchini (about
    1 medium)
$\frac{1}{2}$ cup thinly sliced carrot (about
    1 medium)
2 cups flaked boneless smoked whitefish
    or salmon (about $\frac{2}{3}$ pound)

Cook rotini as directed on package; drain. Rinse pasta in cold water; drain. Mix mayonnaise, yogurt, dill weed, mustard, salt and pepper in large bowl. Add rotini and remaining ingredients except smoked fish; toss. Gently stir in smoked fish.   **4 servings**

SERVING SIZE: 1 Serving 605 Calories (280 Calories from Fat); Fat 31 g (Saturated 5 g); Cholesterol 65 mg; Sodium 500 mg; Carbohydrate 57 g; (Dietary Fiber 3 g); Protein 27 g; *% Daily Value*: Vitamin A 32%; Vitamin C 6%; Calcium 8%; Iron 24%

Fish Terms to Know

Whole fish: Just as it comes from the water

Drawn fish: Whole but eviscerated

Dressed or pan dressed: Ready to cook

Steaks: Cross-section slices, about $\frac{3}{4}$ inch thick, from large dressed fish

Fillets: Sides of fish cut lengthwise away from the backbone—almost boneless

Butterfly fillets: Double fillets held together by skin

Sticks: Cuts from frozen blocks of fish fillets, breaded, partly cooked and frozen

Dilled Pasta Salad with Smoked Fish

Fettuccine-Salmon Salad

1 package (8 ounces) spinach fettuccine
1 cup refrigerated dill dip
1 package (10 ounces) frozen green peas,
  thawed
4 green onions, thinly sliced
1 can (14³/₄ ounces) red or pink salmon,
  drained, skin and bones removed and
  flaked

Cook fettuccine as directed on package; drain. Toss fettuccine, ¹/₂ cup of the dill dip, the peas and onions in large serving bowl. Top with salmon. Serve immediately with remaining dill dip.   **4 servings**

SERVING SIZE: 1 Serving 455 Calories (160 Calories from Fat); Fat 18 g (Saturated 8 g); Cholesterol 120 mg; Sodium 950 mg; Carbohydrate 47 g; (Dietary Fiber 4 g); Protein 30 g; % Daily Value: Vitamin A 6%; Vitamin C 28%; Calcium 32%; Iron 26%

Broiled Swordfish Salad with Salsa

4 swordfish or other medium-fat fish
  steaks, each about 1 inch thick (about
  1¹/₂ pounds)
2 tablespoons olive or vegetable oil
4 cups bite-size pieces salad greens
1 cup chunky salsa
¹/₂ medium papaya, peeled and cubed
  (about 1 cup)

Set oven control to broil. Place fish steaks on rack in broiler pan. Drizzle with 1 tablespoon of the oil. Broil with tops about 4 inches from heat 7 to 10 minutes or until fish is opaque; turn. Drizzle with remaining 1 tablespoon oil. Broil about 5 minutes longer or until fish flakes easily with fork.

Divide salad greens among 4 plates. Top with fish. Spoon salsa over fish; top with papaya.
                                  4 servings

SERVING SIZE: 1 Serving 135 Calories (Calories from Fat); Fat 15 g (Saturated 3 g); Cholesterol 80 mg; Sodium 490 mg; Carbohydrate 8 g; (Dietary Fiber 3 g); Protein 27 g; % Daily Value: Vitamin A 46%; Vitamin C 44%; Calcium 4%; Iron 8%

Marinated Shrimp Kabob Salad

1 tablespoon grated orange peel
¹/₂ cup orange juice
2 tablespoons vegetable oil
¹/₂ teaspoon salt
¹/₂ teaspoon crushed red pepper
2 cloves garlic, crushed
16 large raw shrimp, peeled and deveined
8 ounces jicama, peeled and cut into
  1-inch pieces
1 medium red bell pepper, cut into
  1¹/₂-inch pieces
¹/₂ small pineapple, peeled and cut into
  chunks
4 cups bite-size pieces salad greens

Mix orange peel, orange juice, oil, salt, red pepper and garlic in large glass or plastic bowl. Reserve ¹/₃ cup orange juice mixture; cover and refrigerate. Toss shrimp and remaining orange juice mixture in bowl. Cover and refrigerate at least 2 hours.

Set oven control to broil. Remove shrimp from marinade; reserve marinade. Alternate shrimp, jicama, bell pepper and pineapple on each of eight 10-inch skewers.* Place on rack in broiler pan. Broil with tops about 4 inches from heat about 8 minutes, turning and brushing once with marinade, until shrimp are pink. Place salad greens on 4 serving plates. Top each with 2 kabobs; remove skewers. Serve with reserved orange juice mixture.   **4 servings**

*If using bamboo skewers, soak skewers in water at least 30 minutes before using to prevent burning.

SERVING SIZE: 1 Serving 170 Calories (70 Calories from Fat); Fat 8 g (Saturated 1 g); Cholesterol 55 mg; Sodium 340 mg; Carbohydrate 19 g; (Dietary Fiber 2 g); Protein 8 g; % Daily Value: Vitamin A 14%; Vitamin C 58%; Calcium 4%; Iron 10%

Marinated Shrimp Kabob Salad

Hawaiian Crab Salad

Papaya and mango, both tropical fruits that have become more readily available throughout this country, have sweet, fresh flavors when ripe. Use a grapefruit spoon to scoop out the seeds from the papaya. Take a knife and carefully cut away the mango pulp from the large flat pit in the middle of the fruit.

1 cup fresh or frozen raspberries
1 medium bunch leaf lettuce, coarsely
   shredded
1 papaya, peeled, seeded and chopped
1 mango, peeled, pitted and chopped
2 packages (8 ounces each) frozen salad-
   style imitation crabmeat, thawed
Raspberry Vinaigrette (below)
¼ cup chopped macadamia nuts

Mix all ingredients except Raspberry Vinaigrette and nuts in large serving bowl. Toss with vinaigrette. Sprinkle with nuts. **4 servings**

Raspberry Vinaigrette

¼ cup vegetable oil
2 tablespoons raspberry vinegar
2 teaspoons raspberry jam

Shake all ingredients in tightly covered container.

SERVING SIZE: 1 Serving 365 Calories (180 Calories from Fat); Fat 20 g (Saturated 3 g); Cholesterol 35 mg; Sodium 990 mg; Carbohydrate 32 g; (Dietary Fiber 5 g); Protein 19 g; *% Daily Value*: Vitamin A 32%; Vitamin C 100%; Calcium 6%; Iron 6%

Fish on the Fly

Looking for a quick way to prepare delicious seafood in a flash? Try these fix-it-fast ideas for yummy seafood dishes.

- Use frozen crab/shrimp mixture, thawed, for a quick seafood cocktail. Serve with cocktail sauce and lemon wedges.
- Add leftover cooked vegetable and cooked fish or seafood to prepared cream-based soup for a simple, super chowder.
- Stir any fish or shellfish (canned, frozen or cooked) into your favorite spaghetti sauce or cream sauce and serve over cooked pasta.
- Make sandwich spreads with drained canned seafood (shrimp, crab, clams, salmon, tuna). Mix with mayonnaise, onion, celery and a squirt of lemon juice.
- Use canned or frozen shrimp or crab in stir-fried dishes. Combine with deli or leftover vegetables and teriyaki sauce.

Tangy Shrimp Noodle Salad

2 cups uncooked noodles (about
    4 ounces)
2 cups coarsely chopped zucchini (about
    2 medium)
1/2 cup sliced celery (1 medium stalk)
1/4 cup sliced ripe olives
1 can (4 1/4 ounces) tiny shrimp, rinsed and
    drained
Horseradish Dressing (below)
Salad greens

Cook noodles as directed on package; drain. Mix all ingredients except salad greens. Refrigerate at least 2 hours but no longer than 24 hours. Spoon onto salad greens.

        4 servings, about 1 1/2 cups each

Horseradish Dressing

1 cup plain nonfat yogurt
1/3 cup reduced-calorie sour cream
2 tablespoons prepared horseradish
1 tablespoon finely chopped onion

Mix all ingredients.

SERVING SIZE: 1 Serving 185 Calories (35 Calories from Fat); Fat 4 g (Saturated 1 g); Cholesterol 75 mg; Sodium 220 mg; Carbohydrate 25 g; (Dietary Fiber 2 g); Protein 14 g; % Daily Value: Vitamin A 10%; Vitamin C 18%; Calcium 20%; Iron 14%

Shrimp and Potato Salad

2 1/2 cups cooked small shrimp
2 cups cubed cooked potatoes
1 cup cooked green peas
1/4 cup chopped celery
2 tablespoons lime juice
1 teaspoon ground cumin
1/4 teaspoon salt
1/8 teaspoon freshly ground pepper
3/4 cup mayonnaise or salad dressing
4 tablespoons snipped fresh cilantro
Lettuce leaves
3 tomatoes, cut into wedges

Mix shrimp, potatoes, peas, celery, lime juice, cumin, salt and pepper. Cover and refrigerate at least 2 hours.

Just before serving, toss shrimp mixture, mayonnaise and 3 tablespoons of the cilantro until potatoes are well coated. Serve on lettuce with tomatoes and remaining cilantro.   **6 servings**

SERVING SIZE: 1 Serving 325 Calories (205 Calories from Fat); Fat 23 g (Saturated 4 g); Cholesterol 120 mg; Sodium 400 mg; Carbohydrate 19 g; (Dietary Fiber 3 g); Protein 14 g; % Daily Value: Vitamin A 14%; Vitamin C 40%; Calcium 4%; Iron 16%

Citrus Shrimp Salad

Citrus Dressing (below)
1 package (12 ounces) fusilli (corkscrew
    shape) pasta
3 oranges, peeled and cut into sections
2 grapefruit, peeled and cut into sections
1 package (16 ounces) frozen cooked
    shrimp, thawed

Prepare Citrus Dressing. Cook pasta as directed on package; drain. Mix pasta and remaining ingredients in glass or plastic bowl. Toss with dressing. Cover and refrigerate about 1 hour or until chilled.   **6 servings**

Citrus Dressing

1/3 cup vegetable oil
1/4 cup orange juice
2 tablespoons lemon juice
2 teaspoons grated orange peel
1 teaspoon grated lemon peel
1/2 teaspoon salt

Shake all ingredients in tightly covered container.

SERVING SIZE: 1 Serving 435 Calories (125 Calories from Fat); Fat 14 g (Saturated 2 g); Cholesterol 110 mg; Sodium 300 mg; Carbohydrate 61 g; (Dietary Fiber 4 g); Protein 20 g; % Daily Value: Vitamin A 6%; Vitamin C 100%; Calcium 6%; Iron 22%

METRIC CONVERSION GUIDE

U.S. UNITS	CANADIAN METRIC	AUSTRALIAN METRIC
Volume		
1/4 teaspoon	1 mL	1 ml
1/2 teaspoon	2 mL	2 ml
1 teaspoon	5 mL	5 ml
1 tablespoon	15 mL	20 ml
1/4 cup	50 mL	60 ml
1/3 cup	75 mL	80 ml
1/2 cup	125 mL	125 ml
2/3 cup	150 mL	170 ml
3/4 cup	175 mL	190 ml
1 cup	250 mL	250 ml
1 quart	1 liter	1 liter
1 1/2 quarts	1.5 liter	1.5 liter
2 quarts	2 liters	2 liters
2 1/2 quarts	2.5 liters	2.5 liters
3 quarts	3 liters	3 liters
4 quarts	4 liters	4 liters
Weight		
1 ounce	30 grams	30 grams
2 ounces	55 grams	60 grams
3 ounces	85 grams	90 grams
4 ounces (1/4 pound)	115 grams	125 grams
8 ounces (1/2 pound)	225 grams	225 grams
16 ounces (1 pound)	455 grams	500 grams
1 pound	455 grams	1/2 kilogram

Measurements

Inches	Centimeters
1	2.5
2	5.0
3	7.5
4	10.0
5	12.5
6	15.0
7	17.5
8	20.5
9	23.0
10	25.5
11	28.0
12	30.5
13	33.0
14	35.5
15	38.0

Temperatures

Fahrenheit	Celsius
32°	0°
212°	100°
250°	120°
275°	140°
300°	150°
325°	160°
350°	180°
375°	190°
400°	200°
425°	220°
450°	230°
475°	240°
500°	260°

NOTE
The recipes in this cookbook have not been developed or tested using metric measures. When converting recipes to metric, some variations in quality may be noted.

Index

Page numbers in *italics* indicate photographs.